The Great Abdication

Why Britain's Decline
is the Fault of the Middle Class

Alexander Deane

imprint-academic.com

Published in the UK by Imprint Academic
PO Box 200, Exeter EX5 5YX, UK

Published in the USA by Imprint Academic
Philosophy Documentation Center
PO Box 7147, Charlottesville, VA 22906-7147, USA

ISBN 0 907845 97 5

A CIP catalogue record for this book is available from the
British Library and US Library of Congress

*

Alexander Deane read English Literature at Trinity College,
Cambridge and took a Masters degree in International Rela-
tions as a Rotary Scholar at Griffith University, Australia.
He is a World Universities Debating Champion and is
training to become a Barrister.

*

By the same author published by Imprint Academic

Off With Their Wigs!
Judicial Revolution in Modern Britain

by Charles Banner and Alexander Deane

SDG

Acknowledgements

Peter Hitchins — *il miglior fabbro*

For their thoughts:
  Ben Brafman, Jeremy Brier, Laila De Melo, Ryan Goss, Rowena Grant-Frost, Simon Mollan, Simon Quinn, Michael Sanderson, Ewan Smith, Matt Stadland, Amanda Wolthuizen, my family. This acknowledgment of their insight should not be taken to mean that they necessarily agree with anything herein: indeed, the contribution of many was to provide the polar opposite of my own opinion. Many merits here are theirs, and all faults are mine.

For supplying a safe haven and for the happiest of childhoods:
  my parents.

For endless support, patience and love:
  Dimity Grant-Frost.

For showing me how to be thoughtful:
  Professor Colin Mackerras, Senator Russell Trood.

For inspiring me with a vision of a better way to live:
  The Rotary Foundation

For wisdom and patience:
  my publisher, Anthony Freeman.

*

Elements of Chapter One previously appeared in the 2003 edition of *The Monash Debating Review*, in 'Making "them" do what "we" want: in defence of cultural imperialism.'

Elements of Chapter Three previously appeared at www.debatabase.com in 'Abolishing sex education.'

Contents

The Middle Class

It is to be observed, that the middle class which is universally described as both the most wise and the most virtuous part of the community, the middle rank, are wholly included in that part of the community which is not the aristocratical. It is also not disputed, that in Great Britain the middle rank are numerous, and form a large population of the whole body of the people. The opinions of that class of the people who are below middle rank, are formed, and their minds are directed, by that intelligent and virtuous rank who come the most immediately in contact with them, who are in the constant habit of intimate communication with them, to whom they fly for advice and assistance in all their numerous difficulties, upon whom they feel an immediate and daily dependence, in health and in sickness, in infancy and in old age; to whom their children look up as models for their imitation, whose opinions they hear daily repeated, and account it their honour to adopt. There can be no doubt that the middle rank, which gives to science, art, and to legislation itself, their most distinguished ornaments, the chief source of all that has exalted and refined human nature, is that portion of the community of which, if the basis of representation were ever so far extended, the opinion would ultimately decide. Of the people beneath them, a vast majority would be sure to be guided by their advice and example.

James Mill
1816 'Government' supplement to
The Encyclopaedia Britannica (4th Ed.)[1]

---

[1]   *An Anthology of Pieces from Early Editions of Encyclopaedia Britannica* (London, 1963) p. 8.

Introduction

Are You Middle Class?

I am middle class. My parents are both teachers. They invested in shares when the government privatised our state industries. They own the home I grew up in. I attended a suburban state comprehensive school. We holidayed regularly in Europe. I went to University. I have been covered by a private medical plan. I am going to be a barrister. I think of myself as being middle class.

That satisfies me that *I* am middle class. But who are the middle classes? In his paean *The Decline and Fall of the Middle Class and how it can Fight Back*,[1] Patrick Hutber states that this question has never received a satisfactory answer; he contends that 'the mere lack of a definition has, in a strange way, damaged the middle classes in the past. It is much easier to portray them as a snobbish, selfish minority if one carefully avoids the necessity of asking who they are.'[2]

Why not simply ask people? Why not ask, 'are you middle class?' In 1976, Hutber's concern with such surveys was that social aspiration meant that results were distorted. He thought that there were fewer people in the country who were actually middle class than the number who viewed themselves as such.[3] My concern in 2005 is that there are more. An 'inverse snobbery' is at play in Britain, whereby people that would by most objective standards be considered middle class think of themselves as working class. 'In the last major survey of the issue, two-thirds of all Britons announced that they

[1]   Patrick Hutber, *The Decline and Fall of The Middle Class, and How it Can Fight Back* London, 1976.
[2]   Ibid p. 16. I acknowledge that there is no definitive homogenous group that is 'middle class' and that there is great diversity amongst those that are broadly (and recognisably) 'middle class.' The pedantic phrase 'middle classes' could be used but, following Hutber's example, I shall prefer the simpler 'middle class'.
[3]   Ibid p. 21.

consider themselves to be working class; 55 per cent of social groups ABC1 think that they are working class.'[4] In both Hutber's time and mine, asking individuals to volunteer a position on their status is — whilst interesting for other reasons — not conducive to determining it.

Having discussed various potential standards as measuring tools of class — education, manner of speech, income, occupation; and having dismissed each one, Hutber goes on to settle for *motivation* as his key distinguishing quality — using the word to describe a set of 'virtues, aspirations and attitudes'. This presents difficulties, as it is my contention that that it is this very motivation that has been given up by the middle classes. I believe that these qualities have been largely (and sometimes consciously) abandoned, but that they are in some ways still visible. He believes that being middle class is ultimately 'a state of mind'[5] — but I believe that the state of mind he envisages is a state of mind now consciously shed, disavowed by many in society who would traditionally have been held to be middle class.

One of Hutber's main theses is that the individuals within the middle class distinguish themselves from the class below them by their general willingness to rely on their own endeavours — rather than those of the state — to support them and determine their life's path: proof of his supposition, he suggests, is manifested in the traditional middle class tendency to save for the future, foregoing immediate pleasure for future security and greater pleasure. I believe that this is no longer the case, and that increasingly our middle class looks to the state for guidance in living in a way once seen only amongst our lower classes, which were at least in part compelled so to do by their financial state.

This confusion reflects Judith Brett's conclusion: that discussion of 'the middle class' is difficult because of 'the failure to resolve whether the term middle class is ... part of a schema of social classification Marxist or otherwise, or whether it is a term of self-description. Of course it is and can be both, but it is important in using it to know which is which.'[6] Brett was interested in the latter: in 'the middle class' as a term 'people use to describe themselves:' more particularly, as a 'projected moral community whose members are

---

[4]   John Lanchester 'The rise of the angry young chav' p. 23 *The Daily Telegraph* 30th October 2004.

[5]   Hutber p. 27.

[6]   Judith Brett *Australian Liberals and the Moral Middle Class: from Alfred Deakin to John Howard* (Cambridge, 2003) p. 7.

identified by their possession of particular moral qualities'.[7] I am interested in the way in which these two templates of the middle class once neatly fitted on top of one another in Britain, but now do not.

I will look at the middle class through the former definition: I wish to discuss a category of individuals whose boundaries are determined by general, rule of thumb criteria such as a particular level of income, non-manual occupation and home ownership — the 'I know them when I see them' middle class: broadly speaking, these were once individuals that in effect were also in the Brett *moral* definition of middle class, being people upon whom one could traditionally depend to defend, in their behaviour and in their attitudes, established values and moral standards, but now cannot.

Brett, like Hutber, believes that the middle class 'is not a class defined by its members' economic role, but a class of individuals whose membership of the middle class is the result of their individual attributes and moral qualities'.[8] I wish this were the case, but, in the United Kingdom at least, I do not believe it is, as individuals opt out of the grouping both consciously and by behaviour: given this perspective, discussing the middle class in any way other than as a group identified objectively from 'above', on an abstract, objective basis, would be meaningless.

[7]   Ibid.
[8]   Ibid p. 9.

Chapter 1

The Abdication of Middle Britain

I say there are simple answers to many of our problems — simple, but hard. It's the complicated answer that's easy because it avoids facing the hard moral issues.

Ronald Reagan[1]

The promotion of the common good is a duty incumbent upon all citizens. The Americans enshrined it in the Preamble to their Constitution as the need to 'promote the general welfare'. It is a responsibility once seized upon by the middle class as its raison d'etre. Whilst, broadly speaking, the urge to encourage and assist others through charity and good deeds still remains a characteristic of our middle class, the willingness to chastise and upbraid those who offend against common values, and thus against the common good, does not. Condemnation of wrong is the 'hard part' of the promotion of the common good — the stick, without whose use the carrot is just appeasement.

I shall suggest throughout this work that the decline in middle class willingness to display disapproval and cast judgment on others is mirrored in a decline in civility in British society, as there is no longer a prescriptive norm that shapes our modes of behaviour. Just as there are disagreements as to what exactly constitutes the middle class, there are many different opinions as to what its social function is (or whether it has one at all). In the course of this book, I will outline many responsibilities I believe our middle class currently neglects in failing to promote the common good. But if there were only to be one, it would be this: to be civil. To be civil, and through

---

[1]   As quoted in *The Economist* 'Special Report: the Reagan legacy' 12th June 2004.

word and deed and example to encourage civility in others. In this, our middle class currently fails.

Aristotle said that the best state is one dominated by the middle class.[2] This is true — not only in that the middle class should have control of the state's means of governance, but also in that their *values* ought to dominate the political environment. Since the inception of true representative democracy, this has been the case in Great Britain. That it is untrue now is not the result of an essential change in society's make-up, as such. We still have a middle class — it just doesn't act like one. It accepts all the benefits of its position, but discharges none of the traditionally concomitant responsibilities — the responsibility to encourage, to exert influence, to condemn — to *lead* the society it exists in, to do more than merely occupy space and spend money. In its modern reluctance to perform these rites, it simply reflects the people that make it up: its approach is the me-focus of the individual writ large. And a large segment of the middle class happily adopts the agenda and values of (and votes for) a strange new liberal London set, which openly loathes the middle class that spawned it.

Hutber wrote 30 years ago. His work charted the decline of the middle class and called on it to defend itself, and reinstate itself as the foundation of British society — of its stability and its strength. My contention is that, largely voluntarily, our middle class has abstained from doing so, and that the enormously damaging collapse of our society's norms and standards is largely a result of that abdication of responsibility. Hutber sought to rouse his class to the fight whilst it still could. My outlook, thirty years on, after so much of that fight has been lost, is much more pessimistic.

The Role of Middle Britain

What is the purpose of this book?

To ask this is to ask, what do individuals want to accomplish when they howl, 'something is wrong!'?

I think that there will be many books like this. Many in Britain could write one, if they added together the observations of the wrongs they observe from day to day and tried to explain them. We are trying to explain to one another why we are unhappy.

My answer is that the middle class is not doing its job. I believe that the middle class should wield a controlling influence on soci-

---

[2]   Aristotle *Politics* trans Benjamin Jowett (Kitchener, 1999) p. 95:
      http://www.economics.mcmaster.ca/~econ/ugcm/3ll3/aristotle/Politics.pdf

ety's morality and conscience, in a broadly conservative and judg-
mental way. At the least, it is not pulling its weight. At the worst, it
is at the forefront of dismantling our traditional mores and values at
the very time in which Britain most needs 'the instinctive sanity of
the middle class'.[3]

I seek to begin a discussion. By throwing up my hands and saying, don't do this — think differently, I seek to have people talk
more about the problems I see, and imagine they do too. For ironically, whilst the behaviour of the middle class sets society's tone,
determines its atmosphere, increasingly our political outlook is so
dictated by a narrow, politically intolerant group of supposed 'liberals' (though they are the most illiberal people to hold sway in Britain since Cromwell) that many are afraid to be condemned for the
'incorrectness' of their views, and keep their politics to themselves.
In an environment supposedly more interconnected than ever, we
increasingly live in pockets, and don't discuss these things that
upset us most about the world around us: we think we are alone in
noting these faults and flaws that damn our society. We sit silent,
outlining to no one, other than perhaps our family members, the
way that 'everybody's changing and I don't feel right'[4] — the way
that we can feel our country slipping away from what we believe in.

I seek to start conversations around tables, to encourage a sense of
commonality: commonality in being troubled by the state of Britain
in the first place, and then a commonality in caring enough to be
willing to play one's small part in doing something about it. If that
sense of commonality is to exist once again, individuals should be
more willing to intervene, to say to the ten year old idly tearing off
the seat cover on the bus, 'stop that' — for they will not feel morally
adrift in a world that does not seem to reflect their values, but
instead be sure that others — not just in a philosophical sense, but in
an actual, others-on-the-bus sense — share their unwillingness to
see their community fall apart, and will speak up in support of
them.

Thus in his recent book *Status Anxiety*,[5] Alain de Botton pursued
entirely the wrong line: people should worry *more* about what others think about them, not *less*: we should give more thought to the
opprobrium and judgment of our peers. Status anxiety — concern
about the esteem in which we are held by our fellow man, by fellow

---

[3]   John Galsworthy *The Man of Property* first pub 1906, Heinemann 1946 p. 53.
[4]   Keane 'Everybody's Changing' from the album *Hopes and Fears* (2004,
      Interscope Records).
[5]   Alain de Botton *Status Anxiety* (London, 2004).

citizens — holds society together. If the concern is strong enough, individuals tailor their behaviour to avoid opprobrium, facilitating a community in which the state needs less power to ensure order as the care individuals have about the opinions of others causes them to behave in a more orderly way.

So: we should be *more* willing to reject the behaviour of others, based on standards we hold to be objective, rather than attempting to 'empathise' with them and view their position subjectively. 'Society needs to condemn a little more and understand a little less.'[6] We shouldn't allow out judgments to be distorted by over-empathising — by always trying to see the other point of view — because sometimes there *is* a right answer, and it involves telling someone that they are wrong. Such condemnation must come from conviction that refuses to tailor itself to the whim of fashion or distort itself to allow every perspective to hold sway.

In other words, we should be more prejudiced.

Instead, just at the time when society needs most guidance, we have educated our children to be 'politically correct', positively promulgating the idea that it is wrong to condemn the behaviour of others. We should be doing quite the opposite of this: we should be instilling moral rigidity. People are called 'uptight' or 'old-fashioned' if they attempt to support standards of behaviour that are in society's interests; they are undermined by the very people such standards benefit. This is destructive and wrong. Moral rigidity is a social virtue and should be taught to society's citizens.

The middle class is guilty not merely of the abandonment of these core principles, but also of complicity in their impending utter destruction: for change this total and this swift could not have been accomplished without the middle class actively promulgating it, mocking and sneering at the things it once held dear.

Why is it that the middle class behaves like this? Perhaps, as Theodore Dalrymple suggests, in reaction to the loss of empire and subsequent loss of prestige and sense of purpose, they have 'turned with the ferocity of disappointment on a culture that had first raised its hopes and expectations and then dashed them'.[7] Internally, too, the position municipal power held by the upper middle class in Joseph Chamberlain's day — the ability to control the events and style of the city in which they lived — has in the main died away too. Outside interests control the instruments of commerce and industry

---

[6]   John Major, in interview with the *Mail on Sunday* 21st February 1993.
[7]   Theodore Dalrymple 'The Britain that Died with Her' *The Spectator* 6th April 2002.

that were once held by the town's bourgeoisie. The bank is no longer run by Mr Smith whom everyone knows, but by an imported ladder-climber from the Hong Kong Shanghai Banking Corporation, who'll have disappeared in two years time, and knows it. Without the control of the pillars of its society, and the sense of permanence that that gives, the middle class is denied its main tool in the role it has accrued and held since our emergence from the feudal system — 'tempering the arrogance of the aristocracy, restraining the crudity of the masses'.[8] Perhaps it instinctively feels that loss, and acts in the absence of that role like the sheriff unjustly deprived of his badge, degenerating until he's just another washed-up bum at the bar who used to be somebody.

On the other hand, perhaps the decline of any real mass religious conviction is the crucial factor. Much has been written about the decline of faith in British society (and elsewhere). It seems to me that whilst the two are not necessarily connected, it is undeniably true that during the time in which we have lost faith, we have also lost faithfulness — faithfulness to ideals and aspirations and modes of proper behaviour, to restraint, fiscal prudence, and moral strength, the maintenance of all of which is in the interests of all, even in an entirely secular society. For 'faith, obedience and mercy are social virtues'[9] and they are most often found in one another's company.

It is certainly true that some of the most positive influence the middle class has had on the working class was consciously motivated by faith. Men and women like John Wesley 'exhorted the working class to live upright, respectable, god-fearing lives;'[10] volunteer welfare reformers motivated by faith and by the Christian ethic did so much to improve the conditions of their fellow men in communities across the country. There is no longer any organisation of middle class people that sees as its function the betterment and improvement of the lot of the working poor, of the type so common for hundreds of years in our past.

So the lack of a faith held in common might be one cause. But so might be a kind of communal self-loathing the middle class visits upon itself now, in which many of its members prefer to self-consciously stand outside it and ridicule it than acknowledge that they are part of it, whilst many of those that remain are cowed into

---

[8]   Jan Morris *Trieste and the Meaning of Nowhere* London, 2001 p. 49.
[9]   Alastair Hannay 'Introduction' in Soren Kirkegaard *Fear and Trembling*, translated Alastair Hannay (London, 1985) p. 7. It should be noted that Hannay was positing the position of a figurative other person in that passage, rather than necessarily expressing his own position.
[10]   Roy Hattersley *Songs of Praise* BBC2 18th July 2004.

silence by the absence of group certainty in the rectitude of proper modes of behaviour, and by the relentless mockery of it — a silence in which the few objecting voices still raised are made to sound shrill.

Whatever the cause, there is no doubt that the middle class has pushed aside its customary decorum and restraint. Chapters of this book document the decline of civility and behaviour in British society about which the middle class have not merely abstained from judgment (in itself, a great fault); rather, much of it has participated in it. The night's quota of leering, binge-drinking louts — a dominant force in British town life, broadly speaking unique to this country — is just as likely to contain those who hold down archetypically middle class jobs in computer programming or accountancy as those that have finished a day of manual labour.

Obviously it would be wrong to lay the responsibility for this change solely at the door of the middle class. The lack of moral rigidity is manifested across the social spectrum, and is not confined to any group within it. However, an influential element of that political correctness currently instilled in 'liberal' middle class thinking and in schools is the idea that the behaviour of others cannot be criticized if it is apparently a reflection of their 'culture'. For the argument in favour of moral rigidity to have force, the belief that others may, within their own 'cultural framework', decide rights and wrongs through an 'indigenous moral spectrum' (what the Parekh report termed 'moral pluralism'[11]) must be defeated.

Moral pluralism or 'relativism' is normally posited in international terms — in the differences in laws exercised by or norms exhibited in different countries. The logic of moral relativism is that, since there is no culture-neutral standard for determining universal moral values, moral values are entirely relative to cultures, and therefore nations or groups should develop along their own cultural lines without external criticism or concern.

But in any given society we impose laws on 'our' culture as if 'we' are an intellectually and morally homogenous whole, which of course we are not — but once those laws are passed, citizens have to accept what is held to be 'right'. Why is that construct discarded at a nation's border — surely 'right' isn't stopped by a mountain range, a river, or a line in the sand, laid down by an accident of history? How ludicrous does any system of morality become if it's held to be

---

[11] 'The Report of the Commission on the Future of Multi-Ethnic Britain' part 1: *http://www.runnymedetrust.org/projects/meb/reportPartOne.html*

inanimate outside a sphere of individuals that, broadly speaking, practice its strictures anyway?

Through the concept of 'jurisdiction' the *law* has found ways to slickly justify such a situation, but how is it possible either *logically* or *morally*? Moral relativism is simply cowardice, an unwillingness to face the implications of the fact that other societies do things that are wrong. If we would hold such things to be 'wrong' within our own culture, we should hold them to be wrong per se, if we are to be intellectually honest.

Accepting a kind of moral relativism, in which something held to be abhorrent in 'our' culture is perfectly permissible in 'theirs', undermines the whole concept of law *anywhere*. Humanity can't be divided up into convenient groups in which rights are absolute and vital in some, and utterly disposable in others. How can I impose any laws on you (through every 'legitimate' channel in society, be it court, parliament etcetera) in 'our' country, if you might simply say 'I agree with *'them'* over there — I don't feel represented by *this* right and wrong, but by *that:* you tell me that the two are equal and *they're* entitled to this practice — why aren't *I?'*

One can only arrive at the conclusion that — rather than scattered pockets of rights and wrongs, sprung up through the happenstance of history — there are *absolute rights and wrongs* and that it is our duty, flawed and imperfect as we are, to seek and attempt to practice them, and to promulgate them. Thus, it is wrong that in the West we believe that we have, broadly speaking, determined these absolutes, but through one device or another continue to justify the state of suffering much of the rest of the world's citizenry endure, outside the sphere in which those absolutes are recognised.

Whilst the question of international morality can be no more than touched on given the scope of this book, moral relativism is obviously a destructive philosophy on an intra-national scale. Where in an international sense moral relativism damages the logic of law, domestically it is corrosive. Attempts to 'empower' groups within society by recognizing a right on their part to live in ways forbidden to others is an absurdity. To say this would be trite, if so many did not seem to preach against it: in order for law to work, citizens with different beliefs or individuals arriving in a nation from another culture must accept its laws. More fundamentally, they must accept its mores. They must tailor their behaviour to conform to the way of life of those already there, in return for being accepted into society.

Moral rigidity more conformity and more prejudice are needed across the board: its lack is manifested as much in the peoples whose ancestry can be traced back in these islands for some time as it is in more recent immigrants. My argument may be attacked on many grounds, but 'racism' should not be one of them. Indeed, it is often recent arrivals to the United Kingdom, coming in part because they have a misplaced faith in the decent state of British society, who are most appalled.

I may be accused of encouraging conformity at the cost of individual liberty. But always in society there is the need balance between individual creativity and freedom, and conformity to common ideals. There obviously have to be *some* values important enough to be enforced; otherwise we would live in a state without laws. The question is one of how far individual liberty should be infringed at the benefit of conformity. Furthermore, in Britain it is not individual liberty that has been stretched so much as the extent to which individuals are permitted to act to the detriment of social norms without repercussion.

These social norms must be reinstated by the people that live here, acting as individuals in their own interest and in the interest of the community they live in. To achieve this end, we must first admit — *proclaim* — that we *aspire* to something, for our nation to *be* something, to be *different*. For we are witnessing a societal crisis of confidence. Britain's is a culture that has given up on its aspirations, and her citizens can sense it. Our country no longer aspires to excellence: excellence in policing, in teaching, in caring for the sick, in our armed forces. Once this happens, even mediocrity is only achieved occasionally. We must agree that we wish to be better than we are.

Aspiration and Respectability

'Respectability' is a much-derided quality. Propriety, keeping up appearances, moral opprobrium — these are concepts apparently seen by many as the detritus of a past age. But when respectability is valued, when its worth is such that individuals aspire to them, then these notions guide society. The decline of these values has seen our society decline too.

A great difference between Hutber's frame of reference and mine is the effect of the Thatcher government that occurred between our times of writing. The tremendous rejuvenating effect of Thatcherism contributed enormously to national self-esteem and economic wellbeing. But it did nothing to halt the decline of the power of social opprobrium. More than ever before, in the Thatcher years social mobility was possible (and encouraged) — but those moving failed to adopt the attitudes, mores and lifestyles normally concomitant with their new status.

The huge post-war expansion of state-employed individuals saw people doing jobs, and living lives, which would normally be categorised as middle class. But a large number of such people declined to define *themselves* as middle class, even resenting the label if applied to them. The political atmosphere of the 1980s exacerbated this.

For the first time, the greatest strength of our establishment — its ability to absorb newcomers and convert them to its attitudes — failed. Thatcher-era upwardly mobiles adhered to the outlooks and lifestyles of their old social groups. State-employed middle-income professionals occupied and still occupy their own latently anti-establishment sub-culture. The organic change seen in most individuals moving upwards in society to conform to cultural norms and adopt conventional establishment attitudes, once so natural when 'making something of yourself' was a universal aim and respectability a desirable quality, no longer occurs.

This change is very important. It marks more than a change in outlook; for the outlook of our middle class defines how society feels about itself, and shapes the nature of our country. The retention of lower-class resentment, coupled with a growing cynicism with regard to authority of all kinds, has led to the near-dominance of an anti-establishment sentiment on the part of the middle class that permeates British culture and colours the way the country feels about itself.

This constitutes the end of the community, at least in any traditionally recognisable sense. For when the middle class has given up its faith in society, it sounds a death knell for the way we have lived for so long. The middle has stopped believing in the institutions that protect and define society — the police force, the courts, Parliament, the armed forces. In the United States, a situation akin to this was reached by way of a cataclysmic event — the Vietnam War. And yet their 'faith' — in their Presidency, in their Congress, in their state, in their country — is at heart still stronger than that of the middle in this country. Our great disillusionment came in incremental steps, in slips and little slides so small we hardly noticed, in the half-century since the Second World War.

Society depends on the middle to keep faith with it. Even when we privately acknowledge our doubt — for instance, our fears that the police are not the shining flawless monument to beneficent protection our forefathers painted them as being — the role of the middle is to still *profess* so to do. For it is in that assumption — that assumed faith — that society is able to continue to be governed, to be policed and so forth. This has been turned on its head: the standard attitude now is to profess instinctive *dis*trust of such institutions. The 'middle' cliché our grandparents shared in believing the police were universally hearty, kind men has given way to today's cliché of believing them to be foul and uniformly corrupt.

When the middle class teaches its children that 'the policeman is your friend', society can be policed: taking our lead from the middle, we as a society believe that, broadly speaking, the police act fairly and in the best interests of us all. When the middle accepts the hypercritical view now so common, the institution is fatally undermined, becoming a sad parody of its former self. Denied the support of those who for so long gave it meaning, stumbling uncertainly, struck by those thought to be its friends, the force sinks into the mire and no longer does its job.[12] For a police force is not — should not be — something *imposed on* society; it is something that should grow out of society. It depends on the middle for *moral support.*

This withdrawal is reflected across many of society's manifestations — in our schools, our hospitals, our democratic structures. All of them depend on the middle and all are suffering as a result of its retreat.

Moral support has been withdrawn as the middle class has declined to partake any longer in traditional modes of behaviour. Society's cohesion depends on certain rites — from respect being paid to institutions and the holders of office, and the performance of pleasantries, to the ritual acknowledgment of the holding in common of certain core beliefs. All of such things lack certainty now, because the middle class has changed.

This change is most obviously displayed in the way we address, treat and react to one another, in Britain today. The change is to do with more than simply a decline in politeness, though that is certainly true. It is concerned with the nature of the individual's discourse with the world and one another; it concerns the attitude to authority, particularly to the middle aged that, year after year, does the heavy lifting of society's work. In cultures such as Japan's, the junior reveres the senior as one that has earned respect through

---

[12] Peculiarly, this change has not been reflected in our common myths, reflected in the modern age in the newest version of our eternal storytelling tradition, television: for the police in our books and on our TV screens continue to heroes, whilst in our newspapers, they are villains. This is particularly ironic as interest in detective fiction is a great middle-class occupation.

experience. Such was once the case here. Instead, just as the middle, that should lead, apes the behaviour of the working class, so the middle-aged, who should lead, increasingly join in the cult of youth: British culture revolves more and more around the whimsy of teen performers and 'celebrities', rewarded with our attention not for achievements, but simply for *being*.

This phenomenon is exemplified by the successful TV show *Big Brother*, in which young, relatively attractive, very stupid people live before constantly recording cameras for 10 weeks. We are told that we should be interested in them, in their infantile thoughts and infantile behaviour: and, because those around us are, increasingly we *are* interested in them. Their pseudo-philosophical discussions and midnight gropes are totally tedious in themselves, but because they form a basis for common discussion, they (and other, similarly tedious things) become important when one is seeking a tool to be able to interact with a large segment of society that disowns all but the most trivial of cultural pursuits.

Traditionally, the real cultural pursuits — theatre, art, literature, cinema with any significance — formed such common interest: and they provided not only entertainment, but also moral instruction. Whilst propriety, decency and decorum might be transgressed, they would not be methodically ridiculed and broken down, as now. We have failed to instil an interest in any of these pursuits in most of the population. But individuals still seek moral lessons from the world around them: and now, rather than any example of decency being set, we have only the *Big Brothers* of this world to look to. Reality TV doesn't just reflect reality; it often shapes it. When individuals see others on television swear profusely, smash things, speed away from the police, they often become more likely to do those things themselves. Thus, the example traditionally provided by a functioning middle-aged middle class — of the rewards gained by hard work, of the success to be had in so working whilst conforming to accepted modes of behaviour — is all but absent as the middle fawns on those less productive and less socially beneficial than itself. There seems to young middle-class people to be little incentive in following the abstemious path their industrious parents underwent, when, after all, everyone's more interested in the mores of those who put two fingers up to rules and work anyway.

Many keen to downplay the extent of Britain's social decline make the traditional objection to theses such as mine: they suggest that I point to a halcyon age that never truly existed, and that observations such as mine are not new. This trite old line, constantly spouted by those seeking to undermine negative observations of society's problems has little credibility. Take the example given above, of the destruction wrought by a child on a bus in front of adults. The evidence I see tells me that individuals in society would once have been much more likely to have acted to halt such behaviour than they are now. Just as policemen and teachers were once able to physically discipline errant children and now cannot, the ethos of wider society was once more conducive to intervention in the misbehaviour of the young but now is not, not only because of the removal of the tool of physical chastisement but also of a culture of fear — we fear the repercussions of acting in the litigious age, but also we fear violence from those that once would have been held in check by a culture of respect. The same is true — especially the fear of violent response — in relation to the thuggery and vandalism of adults.

Even if that is in fact not the case, and that this state is nothing new, my concern is how society *should* be. What of it, if others had bemoaned their culture, as I now bemoan mine? Does it mean that observations of the current ills of society are invalid, if similar complaints were made in the age of the mods and the rockers? Indeed, might the problems that others have observed in *that* age, help explain how we have come to our problems in *this* age?

Walpole made much of the apparently dissolute state of his fellow Britons by way of pointing out that 'not half as many coaches attended Chatham's[13] funeral as had attended the actor-manager Garrick's'.[14] Here, we should suppose, is evidence that our cult of the individual, and societally peripheral individual at that, is nothing new.

Indeed, the comparison runs deep, as Walpole also bemoaned 'the general breakdown in law and order, the huge increase in the number of highwaymen and footpads infesting the roads, and the growing permissiveness of a society mad for scandal'.[15] So yes, indeed we have faced such a plight before: but that is not to say that we are guaranteed to overcome it. Rather, the question is, do we have the *strength* to, as we did then? And does not this fascination with the frivolous run *deeper* than it did then? For whilst it is true that this has long been a cultural strand in our national life, that strand in Walpole's time did not on the whole permeate the

[13] The former prime minister William Pitt the Elder.
[14] As quoted in Edward Grierson *The Imperial Dream: British Commonwealth and Empire 1775-1969* London, 1972 p. 33.
[15] Ibid.

thoughtful classes, and most individuals within them had an idea of proportion: it is the *extent* of the modern fascination with the peripheral and concomitant abstention from the realities of life that are so shocking. Walpole's middle-class contemporaries were acutely aware of their place in that world, had opinions on the rightness and rectitude of modes of social behaviour, believed in their ability to shape the world around them through exercising moral judgment. On the other hand, we have given up on trying to shape reality, to give it any sense of moral purpose, and instead content ourselves with recording and watching it: vis *Big Brother,* people sit around doing very little, watching TV footage of people sitting around doing very little.

In our rudderless society, those willing to fill the vacuum left by the absence of a strong middle have instilled the notion that rudeness is a legitimate manner of expression; the ruder one is, the stronger, the more aggressive, and the more successful. This is a step back from all the lessons civilization has gained. Aspiration — the wish to better oneself — is inverted, and individuals 'aspire' to behave badly.

Perhaps even on a conscious level, great swathes of the element in society that has traditionally governed its path have decided that they don't *want* to be middle class. The mimicking of inner city culture, the slurring of accents to form a Creole of sub-lingual 'tribal' discourse in which one recognises another 'alright' person by their similar rejection of proper English, is symbolic of a deliberate effort by some whose parents and upbringing are thoroughly middle class to reject the world of their forebears — and by others, merely an attempt to conform to youth culture around them. In young Britain, mimicry of, specifically, black American ghetto culture has been followed by mimicry of those that adopt that mimicry.

This alienation of the middle class from itself is not new. Hutber wrote in 1976:

> I spent the first twenty-five years of my life in Ealing ... surely, even today, a quintessentially middle-class place ... I derive a warmth and comfort from that background. How strange that I should have thought it necessary to write the preceding sentence. Nobody would regard it as being in the least unusual or out of the way for someone with a working-class background to pay tribute to what it had given him. That it is, alas, more unusual to praise a suburban home rather than, say, a back street in Leeds is an indication of how thoroughly we have all been brainwashed.[16]

---

[16]   Hutber p. 10.

The association of decent standards of behaviour with a reviled class and tradition is tremendously damaging. I am greatly concerned by the rise in crime in Britain, and address it later: but in determining the everyday nature of society, as Edmund Burke wrote, 'manners are of more importance than laws'.[17] The greatest decline in societal wellbeing has occurred in the events, behaviour and discourse that occupy the gap between actual lawbreaking and behaviour that is absolutely without flaw. The way we treat one another would shock many of our forebears from the ostensibly 'less civilised' past. The abandonment of notions of politeness are unique to Britain's middle: 'the middle class of rural Umbria or young clubbers in Madrid observe a social etiquette that is far closer to that of Edwardian London than anything that you will [now] find in this country. Manners are not so readily tainted with snobbery as they are here.'[18]

We have surrendered our provincial town and city centres to an aggressive youth, mob culture; after a certain time, it is neither pleasant nor safe for most people to be in the centre of the town they live in. We are threatened by groups of drunken young men, or accosted by gangs of hooded teenagers, for daring to venture out into our own towns. Resilient, enduring people that we are, it is normally adapted to and not mentioned: if it is pointed out, most commonly by a shocked visitor from abroad, the answer is normally that 'well, that's how it is'. But it is *not* how it is elsewhere, nor should it be here.

Zero Tolerance

Taking action against crime at its most innocuous sends a clear message that illegal behaviour will not be tolerated, reducing the incidence of every level of crime.[19]

If as a culture we allow individuals to swear, to shout, to push and shove, the next level of authority is challenged. There is always an instinct to rebel and desire to transgress (such an instinct is often a symptom of an individuality and non-conformism that is desirable). But raise the bar on what is socially acceptable, and that instinct is aimed at a more significant target. Fail to instil discipline

[17] Burke, Edmund *Selected Works of Edmund Burke* ed. E J Payne, Francis Canavan 1999:
http://www.econlib.org/library/LFBooks/Burke/brkSWv3cl.html
[18] Bella Thomas 'Previous Convictions' *Prospect* February 2003 p. 80.
[19] George L Kelling and Ronald Corbett 'This Works: Preventing and Reducing Crime' *Civic Bulletin*, No 32 March 2003: Center for Civic Innovation at the Manhattan Institute p. 2.

in small things in our children's lives, and they will push and push until a barrier willing to resist them is reached. When this process goes on long enough, society has a large group of people (predominantly, but not all, male) who seem entirely unable and unwilling to exert any control over their own behaviour, and are unceasingly aggressive towards others — including to the weak, the elderly. Such is now the case in Britain.

Society's atmosphere is governed by such attitudes. The air of strong authority makes people less likely to abuse their fellows — likewise, its absence makes such abuse more likely. This authority doesn't have to be one upheld by policing and laws; indeed, attempts to enforce such rules are often counterproductive. Rather, moral opprobrium and peer condemnation are the most effective tools in enforcing cultural behaviour patterns. The refusal of the new middle class to wield these tools has undermined all our traditions and standards. Remove the idea of our fellows' watchfulness and condemnation of transgression, an overarching cultural theme that has been with us since the earliest days of the tribe, and society ceases to be a place in which rules are in force but are exceptionally avoided — a society that is essentially law-abiding — and becomes a place in which laws are abstract and feel as if they are nothing to do with us, and are only arbitrarily applied to those unfortunate enough to come to the attention of a machine far away from us — a society that is essentially lawless.

By way of example: according to the shop workers' union, every minute of every working day in this country a member of shop staff is attacked by a customer.[20] Most frequently, workers are attacked after work, by customers they've refused to serve — by gangs of youths refused alcohol, or cigarettes. In 2002, 16,000 workers were physically assaulted during the course of their work. On average, workers can expect to be verbally abused every three days, threatened every 15 days, and actually attacked once a month.[21] It is lamentable that in modern Britain, people cannot work in sales departments of normal stores free from fear. Whilst obviously wrong, it has always been understood that there is an element of risk in working as a teller in a bank, or as the clerk of a late night store: criminals have traditionally targeted such places. But this more recent phenomenon is not driven by actual criminal intent per

---

[20] 'Every minute of every day, a shopworker is attacked by a member of the public' Union of Shop, Distributive and Allied Workers 29th September 2003: *http://www.usdaw.org.uk/usdaw/news/1064852850_2368.html*

[21] Ibid.

se (that is, for the individual to profit from obtaining stolen goods etcetera), but rather by the uncontrolled aggression prevalent in our tantrum society, where individuals are effectively taught that they will never be told 'no'.

The great overarching crisis in British society is the falling away of authority — be it in our schools with teachers unable to maintain discipline, in our hospitals where even basic standards seem impossible to enforce, or on our streets where our police are unable to stop so much aggression and yobbishness, and much worse. The ability to maintain standards in these places rests on the willingness of society to ascribe to them, and give the support necessary to those appointed to uphold them — a willingness that depends on the middle class. Both these things, the desire for standards and the willingness to enforce rules, are in doubt. Our teachers are undermined by rules that protect the 'rights' of students at the cost of any discipline, and by the automatic support of every claim against them until, after being exposed without defence to many months of soul-destroying assumption of guilt and the battering by the community that goes with it, such claims can be proven wrong. The conscious destruction of the traditional hierarchy in our hospitals has been paralleled by the fall of any real standard of hygiene in the NHS, source of much 'secondary sickness' — conditions (often fatal) caught *after* entering the hospital — as there is no-one to enforce the drudgery of cleanliness necessary to prevent it. The abdication of the middle class from its traditional position as moral supporter of those society delegates to lead has led to the fall of authority in all these arenas.

But that authority once existed in all these places. It can be regained. The petty crime, the litter, the graffiti, the aggression on our streets (and in our lives) and the despondence about our national future, are *not* inevitable. These things are natural products of our national decline, prompted by the failure of our middle class to defend the values and beliefs that hold littering to be wrong, aggression to be wrong, is essentially patriotic and proud of country, and so forth. We must consciously subscribe to standards and support those striving to uphold them. Decline is not irresistible.

We must teach people to be prejudiced once again. The place to start is education.

Chapter 2

The Root of the Abdication: Education

The decline of Britain's educational establishment has occurred in tandem with the falling away of traditional middle class values. Hard work, a willingness to learn from authoritative source, a belief in and support for excellence — these are all virtues that character-ised the middle class of two generations ago, particularly in its approach to education.

To the detriment of British students, 'education is the last redoubt of socialist beliefs'.[1] Our children no longer learn. They do not receive instruction. Rather, they are encouraged to experience and learn from that experience, despite the fact that children don't have the set of pre-learned values and filters necessary to gain anything from such a method of 'education'. In the name of child-centric edu-cation, we have abandoned long-held principles of teaching. British children have little conception of what are traditionally the absolute basics: the rudiments of grammar and elemental mathematics. This is not because today's children are stupid. It is because they are being taught in a stupid way.

We learn by taking on challenges, and overcoming them: we learn by being tested, *truly* tested. When we do not challenge our children, we betray them: we have ceased to educate, and begun to indulge:

> Problems are the cutting edge that distinguishes between success and failure. Problems call forth our courage and our wisdom. In fact, they create our courage and wisdom ... when we desire to encour-age the growth of the human spirit, we challenge and encourage the

[1]   'Few are chosen' *The Economist* 3rd July 2004.

human capacity to solve problems just as in school we deliberately set problems for our children to solve.[2]

Or rather, *should* set problems for them to solve, but don't. This unwillingness in the teaching establishment to actually *teach* anything reveals a wider philosophy of life in Britain, one being passed on to our children without our consent: individuals should be able to do as they please, and never be challenged.

Without being challenged, and without a certain element of instruction by rote, children do not learn. Things that aren't natural to individuals — such as a knowledge of times tables — can become instinctive through socialisation. Indeed, such things *can't* be learned without being imparted by others. An understanding of nouns and verbs does not leap unbidden into the head of a child — it has to be put there.

Given that we *can* ensure that individuals emerge from schools with a corpus of knowledge, we ought to (how surprising past generations would find it that one has to make this argument at all). The obvious question is, *what* should be taught, not *whether* we should teach.

Asking what should be taught underlines the existence of the possibility of control: there is a choice, and this choice can be conscious — it is *our* choice to be made, and not the spawning of a tidal social pull. Nor is it the case that all potential choices are of equal merit, are equally good or bad. The individual needs *instruction*: in subjects — in English, in Science, in Mathematics; and also more generally — in manners, in behaviour.

In much of India, in the Caribbean, in many African countries, the traditional British system has been maintained — a rigorous insistence on grammar and arithmetic, underpinned by an understanding that some things (such as times tables and basic rules of language) must be learned by rote. The result, despite scant resources and class sizes often twice that seen even in understaffed schools in this country, is a more educated and more versatile population in those countries, swifter to adapt to new challenges such as the IT boom and more equipped to answer typical questions posed by the world of employment. Lessons learned stay with them for life — as they once did with our own children, instructed in this way.

Instead, our schools encourage children to 'learn for themselves'. It is perfectly obvious to most of us that children's grasp of times tables has declined since the abandonment of traditional teaching by rote, and the evidence (in the form of research conducted by

---

[2] M. Scott Peck *The Road Less Travelled* New York 1978.

Royal Holloway University[3]) supports this: but this practice has nothing to do with evidence. The practice is instead based on a set of deeply held political beliefs held by many in the educational elite. They are opposed to values that prize the guaranteed bestowal of knowledge above the notion that the child should discover things without being told them.

The retention of those values elsewhere does not connote an imperialist or colonial hangover, but rather a sensible retention of a beneficial element of the colonial experience. In the small museum beside the jetty for the ferry to Robben Island, where Nelson Mandela and his fellows were imprisoned for so many years by the Apartheid regime, exercise books are exhibited from lessons prisoners taught one another in grammar, comprehension, algebra. These lessons, regularly tested by rigorous examinations (often failed), are recorded in remarkably cramped writing; an effect of the fact that paper and stationery were scarce and resources were often deliberately withheld. Nevertheless, it is clear to any observer that the standard sought and obtained is a great deal higher than our classrooms see today.

Rules of grammar, times tables, the periodic table — these aren't prisons imposed on the mind; rather, they are 'mental maps'.[4] They are short cuts, and the possession of them helps the individual find his way with more ease. Once learned, they are lifelong tools, fashioned to help one get something *right*.[5] They are empowering.

Whilst young, children should be taught by rote. When older, when minds are more fully developed and trained, and able to engage with complex concepts and conflicting evidence, they should be taught to use their imagination. We have exactly the reverse procedure. We ask children to discover for themselves

---

[3] 'Reciting times tables is better than counting' p. 6 *The Daily Telegraph* 9th September 2004 drawing on research by Dr Sylvia Steel. The research showed that the trend away from rote learning may actually lead to further results contrary to its aims: the self-confidence of children is undermined by the new practice, too.

[4] Melanie Phillips 'Why I am a Progressive' *New Statesman* January 2000: *http://www.melaniephillips.com/articles/archives/000041.html*

[5] The decline of 'proper' teaching is particularly peculiar as the British possess an innate desire to get things right. The astronomical sales of *Eats, Shoots and Leaves* for example reveals both the British fascination with detail and getting said detail right, and also a converse fear of getting things wrong, of displaying ignorance by doing so — and a vicarious delight in the mistakes of others. In such an environment, not having such knowledge marks one out as lacking.

when young, and then teach by spoon-feeding when the exams come round at senior level.

Equality — Downward

Many in the middle class, whose advantaged families benefit from good comprehensives in market towns and leafy suburbia, call for an equal educational system for all. The effect of such egalitarian efforts is to deprive those in inner cities without such advantages the chance to escape the truly terrible schools in their area. We must puncture the great myth — a fallacy still preached in our educational system today despite the stunningly obvious evidence to the contrary — and proclaim that all comprehensives are *not* the same, nor anything like it. In fact, they are so different from one another as to constitute different classes of schools, just as divisive as the grammar and secondary modern system so derided by educational 'reformers' — the division is into good and bad, with the latter ever growing. Given the effect of 'selection by postcode', it is the children of the poorest who suffer most from the result of the failed experiment the middle class has encouraged.

The pernicious social phenomenon that was 1960s liberalism swept from the family environment the impulse to teach our children about their responsibility to other people (there wasn't anything unique about the thinking of the young in the 1960s: the unique thing was that supposedly sensible people listened to them). At this point, we needed our schools to fill the gap — school was the only possible alternative place to provide that backbone of social interaction. But at that very moment, our educational establishment was undergoing a revolution of its own, with the ascendancy of 'discover yourself' teaching undermining not only the willingness to instruct with regard to subjects, but also the willingness to prescribe moral behaviour. School was no longer about that, it seemed.

As the tendency to question and challenge authority has spread through Britain's middle class, so discipline in the country's schools has become increasingly undermined. The unwillingness of many schools to enforce any meaningful form of discipline is in part a result of the modern litigation culture, and of the lack of support extended to teachers in the face of claims of abuse made by students. Indeed, 45% of teachers leaving the profession cite disruptive student behaviour as one of the main reasons for doing so.[6] This obviously makes instilling any sense of respect difficult — as teachers

---

[6]   James McLeod 'Bollocks to that, sir' pp. 42–47 *Prospect* September 2003.

retreat, and as pupils see that teachers can be forced out. This situation was made worse by David Blunkett's decree in 1997[7] that expulsions should be reduced by a third, effectively leaving some schools powerless in the face of the worst student behaviour. This has worsened to the point at which there is an attack on a teacher every seven minutes of the working school day.[8]

But the challenges made to authority are also a result of the increasing trend on the part of middle class parents, who could generally once be relied upon to support the authority of teachers, to challenge the methods and decisions of members of staff, a tendency that naturally impinges disproportionately on the teaching of those few teachers willing to at least attempt to assert authority and discipline in our schools, as they are correspondingly more likely to attract the ire of the student who wishes to play up. In modern Britain, parents who could once have been relied upon to support schools in instilling discipline constantly assert the 'rights' of the child. The rights to be an individual and not be restrained, even to the extent of damaging the educational experience of those around him.

Put most directly, thanks to the support of parents for the misbehaviour of children rather than for the teacher that seeks to discipline them, it is no longer an accurate generalisation to say that middle class children are better behaved than working class children. Both are equally disruptive, uncontrolled and aggressive in today's schools. Furthermore, better behaved children — often, though obviously not always, the children of the middle class — could once be traditionally relied upon to exert a positive influence on their misbehaving peers, by voicing unhappiness with their behaviour or displaying a reaction that ensured the appropriate stigma was attached to acts of disruption. Increasingly, this is not the case: whether it is due to fear, or to the lack of a sense of duty, good children tend to retreat and 'look after their own' rather than influence their environment.

Disruptive pupils do not only destroy their own education. In a system unwilling to take proper disciplinary action, they hold the success or failure of their classmates in their hands, too. Obviously, the attention of staff is distracted from teaching so less learning is done. Moreover, students whose behavioural inclination in the

---

[7]   Ministry of Education Circular 10/99.
[8]   'Enough is Enough: NASUWT campaign against violence, abuse and harassment' NASUWT 8th January 2004:
       http://www.nasuwt.org.uk/Templates/Internal.asp?NodeID=70334

middle ground between well behaved and awfully behaved — the students whose behaviour is really the mark of a school — have an example set at one extreme, and are drawn to it. The difference between a good class and a bad one can often be the inclusion of only one or two children, whose lead the rest follow. Without them, or with them present but properly disciplined, the students in the middle ground follow the example of their well-behaved peers. With them present and unrestrained, many will ape their behaviour and behave badly too. Every school has some bad children. One does not judge schools by their presence, but rather by the way in which the school deals with them.

Competition

The abolition of competition from our state schools has been fundamental in undermining individual confidence and the kind of rigour, the kind of robustness, from which the British middle class has benefited for so long. Once, many state schools divided students up into houses: the house system and all that went with it was meant to foster bonding, teamwork, and a sense of competitiveness. In this, the state sector was consciously aping our public schools. This was abandoned, and the idea of adopting anything from the private sector was considered laughable — which is regrettable as they have consistently been successful, perhaps the most successful in the world. We are told that the educational establishment has realised the error of its ways. The government's ominously named 'five year plan' announced that it intends to restore the house system in state schools;[9] whether this is an idea born of realisation of the blatant failure of the liberal notions of teaching, or of the fact that the house system has been popularised by the wildly successful *Harry Potter* series of books, can only be guessed at. Whether it actually happens, given the continuing opposition offered by a section of the teaching world to all things competitive, remains to be seen.

As the rates of obesity skyrocket — one in five 15 year old children is clinically obese, according to a House of Commons Select Committee report[10] — the number of traditional sports days at state schools has declined: 'about half'[11] of schools hold no such events in the school year, fearing the effects on children of the 'trauma' of los-

[9]   Richard Garner 'Houses help reduce the trauma of 'big' school' Education *The Independent* 9th July 2004.
[10] Maxine Frith 'Not-so-super sized: sweet makers say big bars must bite the dust' *The Independent* 27th September 2004.
[11] 'Bring Back Sports Days' *The Metro* 12th July 2004 p. 8.

ing. Moreover, physical instruction has diminished, as schools fear the cost of personal injury cases. In the early 1990s, the French declared that the state would fund sporting academies and aim to develop coaching systems to detect and encourage excellence in the athletes of the future. This laudable notion was based in three aims: to improve the nation's sense of self, to promote the image of France abroad, and — as a by-product of the search for the excellent, since all undertake more exercise in the process — to improve public health.

Over the period since, the French have developed from sporadic success to high-level performance in team sports, culminating in winning the rugby and soccer world cups, whilst continuing their traditional success in winter sports.

Meanwhile, British schools have seen sports fields sold off at a truly astonishing rate. Even since 1998, after the proverbial horse had bolted, when the government pledged to end the sale of fields by centralising control of them, sales have continued at a very high rate.[12] Simultaneously, within the schools the very idea of competition and excellence is run down, for it is supposedly elitist to encourage children with a particular aptitude — leaving an absurd reliance on privately educated children becoming our elite athletes as, generally speaking, only in such schools does any real challenging training take place, and only there does the ethos of competition exist to the extent necessary for excellence. Year after year, after exceptional events such as the 2003 Rugby world cup or the 2004 Olympics, our government attempts to insinuate itself into the occasional success yielded by our beleaguered and underfunded athletes, seeking to gain by association with success –whilst constantly running down the ability of the state to train the athletes on which future successes will depend.

This is much the same in the other non-core, creative subjects: in art, in music, in drama, children are not driven to excel in the state sector (indeed, the number of students even *taking* these subjects is declining). The government's 'flagship' specialist schools do nothing to repair the damage, since they are now specifically *discouraged* from selecting students who are gifted in their specialisation as that

---

[12] In the period October 1998–October 2003, 213 applications for the sale of fields were made and only six were rejected. National Playing Fields Association 'Baton Passing on playing fields' 26th September 2003: *http://www.npfa.co.uk/content/newsarticle/77/index.html*

would be unfair.[13] The very raison d'etre of specialist schools, to encourage their specialised subject, has been kneecapped.

The middle class doesn't really seem interested in objecting to this. Perhaps this is natural, since artistic pursuits and the sports in which Britain continues to excel — rugby, sailing, shooting, rowing, equestrianism and so on — are those in which middle class parents pay to have their children privately coached, normally in private schools. How frustrating it must be for the government, having to embrace these living symbols of the refusal to accept the state's levelling-down chokehold on education!

But, whilst the irony must please, the middle class should appreciate that this is short sighted. The demolition of the ethos of competition is bad news for them as much as for everyone else. Whilst it may give some of their children a short term advantage on the sports field, the concert hall, the art gallery or the stage (because there's no working class competition in their fields, and no success in others to detract attention) in the long term something more important — Britain's productivity and strength — is in danger, as the competitive ethos is driven out of students who then limp into the workforce. And in any case, as competition continues to be crushed in the state sector, and the lack of it becomes the norm, the prospect of its destruction in the private sector by regulation becomes ever more likely.

Ultimately, the removal of competition from education is disastrous beyond sport and the immediately related areas — it's disastrous for British society as a whole. For success without failure has no real meaning. Students who are never challenged or tested become complacent and lazy adults. When the teaching environment treats tests as the measure of its own systems — in which results are the judgment of its own 'progress' (and thus must display relentless 'improvement') rather than a method of telling able from not-so-able — individuals are artificially cushioned from the very real and very useful fear and trauma of failing. Coupled with the removal of any meaningful competition from the non-academic areas of educational life, the result is the diminishment of British potential as our adult population are less well-equipped than their counterparts educated rigorously elsewhere.

---

[13] 'Failing the Test' *The Daily Mail* p. 14 30th September 2004.

The Grammar School System

On the whole, the grammar school system was (and where it survives, is) excellent. It is true that the traditional structure of education offered too narrow a spectrum of opportunities, cutting some academically-minded pupils off from an environment in which they would have flourished: but this meant that *more* grammar schools should have been built, not fewer. Even in an environment that saw some under-provision, grammar schools offered bright poorer students the opportunity to be educated to a very high academic standard: the deciding factor was ability, not money. In the drive for 'equality', pushed for by the liberal middle class as it argued for the comprehensive system, that opportunity has been removed. Now, outside of those areas that have retained grammar schools, decent education is provided in two places: some leafy suburban comprehensives, attendance at which is dictated by postcode (and thus by house price), and in private education. So the drive for equality has resulted in an educational system in which the deciding factor is money, not ability.

Evidence for this comes from the one element of 2004's astonishingly 'good' exam results that the government would have us ignore. Northern Ireland's grade A to C GCSE average is an enormous 11% higher than England's.[14] Indeed, the province normally produces better results than the rest of the United Kingdom at both GCSE and A level, which is all the more remarkable because 99.8% of students are educated in the state sector, whilst results elsewhere are buoyed up by an over-performing independent school sector. The success of Northern Ireland's school system is reflected in the fact that it has 'the best record of sending children from disadvantaged backgrounds to university, at 41.3 per cent'.[15] Clearly, something is being done very well by the state system in Northern Ireland: so why doesn't the Government want to trumpet it?

Whilst it is true that the fortunate province has a more traditionalist way of life with a vastly lower divorce rate, ensuring that more students come from stable families, the larger cause of this higher achievement is the fact that Ulster has retained the 11-plus and grammar school system. The benefits of rigour could not be clearer, on the government's own evidence. The government's response to

---

[14] 'Ulster's top of the class' Editorial, p. 19 *The Daily Telegraph* 26th August 2004.

[15] John Clare 'Seventeen Universities face financial penalties for failing to be "inclusive"' p. 4 *The Daily Telegraph* 30th September 2004.

this is to announce plans to abolish the Ulster 11-plus in 2008.[16] Long ago, the liberal educational establishment set itself an absurd and incredibly destructive aim: all must be equal. Squashing those doing better is the easiest way to achieve that aim.

Moving the Goalposts

The fact that pupils fail examinations is not to be lamented. It should be applauded, as a reasonable proportion of failure indicates rigour. An examination that nobody ever fails is absurd. However, the teaching establishment doesn't seem to believe this. It has reacted to failure in two ways — by making examinations easier, and by introducing coursework.

Coursework, now widespread, is a joke. It is symptomatic of the stress parents and teachers put on results obtained rather than what is actually learned by students. The middle class favours it, as middle class parents care enough to chivvy their children night after night, and care enough to help their children cheat. For coursework is often done by parents, by friends. The Internet makes it much easier (and often large chunks are cut and pasted and handed in and rewarded with high marks, only seldom caught). If that were not enough, the whole structure of teaching coursework is complicit in undermining the idea of learning something from it, as multiple drafts are submitted and returned with 'suggestions' for the next draft — that is to say, students are spoon-fed stage by stage to a decent mark. What contributions students themselves actually make in this process is questionable.

One can hardly blame teachers for their involvement in such corruption, given the pressures placed on them by league tables and targets. Every year results are expected to improve, regardless of the ability of the particular year concerned. There's never a ceiling on the level of results considered to be reasonable. Teachers are pushed to obtain 'value-added' results, with students outperforming previous marks and predicted grades. Jobs depend on the results of students. If the student isn't working hard enough, is it surprising — given that failure is 'unacceptable' — that the teacher fills the gap?

Examinations are essentially safe methods of testing, occasionally open to corruption. Coursework is innately open to corruption, though an occasional student is foolishly honest enough to do it himself. We should abandon it altogether.

---

[16] 'Ulster's top of the class' Editorial, p. 19 *The Daily Telegraph* 26th August 2004.

Grade Inflation

It is commonly known that the grades awarded at school level are becoming increasingly meaningless. This long-held belief has now been confirmed by research conducted by Coventry University, which found that a student that failed maths 'A' level in 1991 would receive a B today.[17]

In 1984, 9.3% of A level results were A grade — in 2004, 22.4% were.[18] This is the highest ever proportion, part of a continuous 20 year upward trend. It is matched by GCSE results, which are the best ever, with 58.1% of results grades A–C.[19] In fact, examination results at *all* stages turned in best ever results this year: A levels, GCSEs, seven, 11, 14 year olds and AS levels.[20]

But it is a farce to maintain that the current generation of students is the best educated in history (though, incredibly, this is the Government's explanation). In fact, standards are depressingly low: indeed, teachers and examiners increasingly say so in public — even terming the A level system, the supposed gold standard of secondary education, to be bankrupt.[21]

Part of this bankruptcy stems from the questions being easier. Even more simply, part of it results from reducing the number of correct answers required. At GCSE in 2004, one examining board, Edexcel, awarded 'A' grades to students scoring 45% in their examination. Another, OCR, awarded C grades in French for students scoring 16%.[22] Obviously this leads to higher grades, which seems to be the desired result. *Half* of all students taking maths GCSE achieved an A grade.[23] It doesn't seem to matter to the government that the students actually *know* less. Indeed, parliament was told in expert evidence in 2003 that 'there has been a steady decline in basic skills in mathematics'.[24] Whilst the situation in maths is particularly

---

[17]   'Hard Numbers' *The Economist* 17th April 2003:
       http://www.economist.com/world/europe/displayStory.cfm?story_id=1718799
[18]   Tony Halpin 'Tutors struggle to sift the exceptional from the elite' *The Times* 19th August 2004 p. 25.
[19]   John Clare 'GCSE results crown a record year' *The Daily Telegraph* p. 1 26th August 2004.
[20]   Ibid.
[21]   Patricia Voute 'Grade inflation exists: I should know, I was an examiner' *The Times* 19th August 2004 p. 16.
[22]   Both examples from 'GCSE A-grades for just 45 per cent *The Daily Telegraph* 18th September 2004.
[23]   Chris Woodhead 'Answer the Question' p. 11 News Review *The Sunday Times* 26th September 2004.
[24]   Professor Carol Taylor Fitz-Gibbon (University of Durham) giving evidence before the Parliamentary Education Select Committee 7th April

acute, this is symptomatic of the state of education across the curriculum.

Two problems emerge: it is impossible to really tell how able students are, and really gifted students are not challenged in any meaningful way (if really performing well anyway, they are punished as there's no way of distinguishing their performance from the less impressive entries that still comfortably receive A grades). The simple truth of the matter is something government is totally unwilling to express — fewer students should receive 'A' grades. Logically, therefore, fewer currently receiving Bs should receive those, and so forth: and some candidates currently passed by the exam boards should be failed.

Sideways measures to plaster the absurd situation include the current suggestion that students should also submit a dissertation, as a way of providing more rigour in testing — the aim, as expressed by the Minister for School Standards, David Milliband, being to provide 'new opportunities for the most able young people' without 'shifting the goalposts so more people are downgraded'[25] — so the government's position is that it is unwilling to ensure that grade boundaries of real meaning are enforced, as fewer people would get high marks; but a solution will be provided for the failure to challenge the most able. Thus, the government's express policy is to only address half the issue of grade inflation: the failure to challenge the best students, and concomitant impossibility of perceiving excellence when over a fifth of all candidates are awarded the highest mark, is addressed by providing extra elements for consideration, rather than — as one might think logical — making the examinations more rigorous. It openly permits the other half of the problem to continue: it apparently believes that huge numbers of students getting high grades, which then become devalued, is desirable.

Whilst bemoaning this publicly, the middle class rather likes this situation as its children get better marks. But this approach is essentially short-termist and blinkered, as businesses, employers and the wider world are aware of the situation (every candidate has a raft of seemingly impressive results) and adjust their methods of judging candidates as well as they can to compensate. The more important question should be: are they actually learning anything? Better to

2003 (para 191): *http://www.parliament.the-stationery-officer.co.uk/cgi-bin/ukparl_hl?DB=ukparl&STEMMER=en&WORDS=free%20softwar%20&CO LOUR=Red&style=s&URL=pa/cm200203/cmselect/cmeduski/uc513-ooo/uc51 302.htm*

[25]   Voute op cit.

get a C under a rigorous and respected system, and to actually have gained from the process of education, than be an ignorant 'A' grade student.

The behaviour of the middle class in relation to secondary education has been a disgrace. Having been complicit in the destruction of proper state education by accepting the absurd aim of total equality and comprehensiveness in our children, and permitting through inaction — or positively encouraging — the current lack of any proper teaching, the middle class now increasingly pays to have its children educated — either with tutoring (one quarter of all state school children are now privately tutored[26]) or entirely in the private sector, leaving only the children of the working class to suffer the result of its hypocrisy as they cannot afford to avoid our failing schools.

Higher Education

There are too many people at university today, and they are going there for the wrong reasons. The pushing into higher education of so many children entirely unsuited to it is one of the most damaging policies adopted by the British government. It undermines the ethos of our universities. It damages the currency of a degree. It encourages our youth — of every class — to waste three years on a 'qualification' that will be of little use to them, and to incur immense amounts of debt for the privilege. It is a colossal waste of public money, especially given the very high drop-out rate that naturally follows when young people who should not go to university are presented with it as the only option and natural thing to do, regardless of academic bent. It is little more than a veil on unemployment, as it staggers by up to three years — or even longer — the period before such students affect the jobless figures.

Universities are or should be about instructing a really quite narrow spectrum of individuals in academic subjects, at a high, extremely challenging level. It is a form of education suitable for instructing quite a limited number of careers, although those careers tend to be disproportionately influential in society, rendering the quality of such teaching particularly important. Universities fulfilling this role have existed for many hundreds of years, with the expansion of the sector seen with the advent of the redbrick univer-

---

[26] Geraldine Hackett 'Tutoring soars for state pupils' *The Times* 19th September 2004.

sities being a sensible reflection of the growth of population and economy. The new wave of universities is very different.

There are too many universities in Britain. This country can sustain, at the most, perhaps 20 really academic universities. When one says that far too many people are going to university, perhaps it is more accurate to say that they are going to the wrong kind of tertiary education. The lamentable destruction of the polytechnic system, which carried out work of much real, practical value, has led to the creation (most commonly by the conversion of polytechnics) of 'universities' teaching those whose academic inclination would in the past have been thought insufficient to warrant a university education. Bluntly, academia is not for everyone, and should not be for everyone. Rather, it should be regarded as being for a narrow band of people who are inclined by nature and aptitude to its strictures and challenges — strictures and challenges, which are, in turn, of narrow meaning and value themselves. To widen the group of those going is to diminish the quality of both university and student, to undermine the meaning of achieving each stage in academia, and to encourage many that should not attend to waste their time and money.

The most common criticism of the new institutions comes in the popular press in the form of mocking particularly peculiar courses. However, the advent of new courses is frequently a rather good thing; at least many of them are vocational and lead to good prospects of employment. A degree in hotel management may be overlong and overly academic, but it has a clear point and clear benefits. Rather, the real damage to education comes when weaker universities attempt to teach standard academic degrees such as English or History. These courses are almost inevitably taught poorly, to a poorer standard of candidate. Whilst there are good reasons for a good candidate to go to a generally poor university to take (for example) the Marine Biology degree for which it is justly renowned, there are no good reasons for a good candidate to go to a poor university to take a standard subject degree.[27] Thus candidates that

---

[27] The sole problem with this logic is the case of the good candidate who has botched his 'A' levels. This is rare, since the standards of our A levels are so low. But where it does happen, it is indeed an argument against this position: or might seem to be. First, our friend should be ready to take responsibility for the situation he finds himself in, rather than cry for the change of the system that judges him. After all, he sat the A level exam, and his plight is not a good enough reason to justify the massive expansion of our university sector. But more importantly, would he not be better served by retaking his examinations, and perhaps get into a good university after

could not get in to a good university, and previously would not have gone to university at all, take those places. What do such people gain from their time? There are several traditional replies. Firstly, 'they learn how to learn' — perhaps this is true, though with minimal course requirements teaching to a standard perhaps (or perhaps not) akin to a not very challenging A level course, even this vague aim is often not the case since little has actually had to be learned. Secondly, 'they improve their job prospects' — this is almost certainly not true, as the sheer number of people going to university has forced employers to operate an informal rule of thumb rating of universities to distinguish between candidates (and such ratings often based on eccentric and/or outdated criteria): few employers are impressed by a standard degree from a bad university. Also, in order to calculate this benefit one should also factor in the three years (or more) experience in the workplace they would have but for having gone to university. On the other hand, they generally have a truly alarming level of debt (which typically they will carry into their thirties).

For most students at most universities, whilst time has been spent enjoyably, when judged by their position on leaving the actual results of their investment of money and time are therefore often negative. Crucially, the process has often shaped their attitude to work in the future in a damaging way, too. Having spent several years completing (or not) an unsuitable and unchallenging degree, they are effectively untrained, both unwilling to work and unable to approach most of the tasks that would make them useful additions to the workforce. Often, even those successfully taking up careers find that the most significant effect of their time at university was to lose time on the career ladder: they are behind their contemporaries in experience and must pick up skills once in employment, just as they could have done three years previously, had they not gone to university at all.

In a society that encourages children generally to be unrealistic about their world and their prospects, the time students spend in 'academia' adds to the idea that many jobs are 'beneath them' — most typically, the jobs their parents have performed in order to sustain them. Particular subjects seem almost deliberately designed with this effect in mind, as perceptive observers realised almost two

---

all, rather than going to a poor university which will presumably fail to challenge or fulfil him? A situation in which a few people having to take another year to get good A level grades and thus getting into good universities is preferable to the enormous expense of maintaining our ludicrously large university sector.

decades ago, 'huge numbers of students are being influenced by the biased one-sidedness of contemporary sociology. They are being systematically de-skilled for effective work and trained to be nothing better than critical saboteurs'.[28]

This is not the fault of the students, who know no better. They have done what they have been told to do — they live in an environment in which going to university is the norm, and only failures don't. It is their parents and their schools that should guide them, but do not. All too late, this becomes vividly apparent to parents in the most literal sense of 'coming home to roost' — the prolonged, post-university childhood, in which the new graduate — effectively having no training, but a lack of willingness to work in large sectors — moves back in to the family home at a time their parents had expected to be free of the burden of keeping them at last. Twentysomethings are living at home longer than ever today;[29] finding themselves at an adult age, they lack career skills, no real experience in any job, and little motivation to find or begin one. Their reaction is an extension of that seen in many schools — a resentment of the society around them, and a wordless, raging anger with it.

This is apparent to anyone that travels, and realises that this malaise is hardly inevitable as, whilst it might exist in portions of other nations, in no country other than Britain does it dominate cultural life. Most of all, because they live in countries in which this is not the case, visitors to the United Kingdom are shocked by what they find. As an Australian acquaintance wrote to me:

> Oz is a more positive place … here [in the UK], people are either chronically negative about their prospects OR think the world somehow owes them a living. People have pretty much given up on hoping that anything will improve.

The greatest contribution the middle class has made to this uprooting of our very good educational system — apart from failing to vote against those that executed it (but then, who stood up for it?) — is the effective ending of the willingness of young middle class people to go into business at a junior level upon leaving school, and working their way up a management structure — often choosing not to do so on the advice of their parents, and their schools. Univer-

---

[28]   Professor David Marsland Quoted in *The Observer: Sayings of the Eighties* ed. Jeffrey Care (London, 1989) p. 40.

[29]   Giles Hatersley 'Generation Hopeless goes home to mummy' p. 5 News Review *The Sunday Times* 15th August 2004.

sity is 'what everyone does,' so the majority drift into it. It should not be what everyone does.

The Decline of Practical Skills

This has been simultaneously accompanied to ill effect by the decline of the practical elements of the educational system, too. We have seen the end of the apprenticeship system, the end of a culture that believes in learning a trade. School children are taught plenty of subjects of no real worth, but nothing about the traditional skills — woodwork and metalwork, cookery — that once formed the core of British non-academic teaching. The results of it are obvious in the most basic sense. Almost everyone has a story to tell about a time they had a problem that required an electrician or plumber, but could not find one. Britain is traditionally a high-skills country. This is because practical skills were once unashamedly taught to pupils who were not of an academic bent, and were taught to an extremely high standard. They have disappeared from the curriculum in any meaningful sense in a single generation.

Simultaneously, children acquire through school and through contempt for many jobs that (with a different mindset) they could perform and gain satisfaction from. Ours is a country with many citizens eminently suited to manual work, with many manual jobs available, where those that are so suited have been 'educated' out of contemplating such work themselves, have been taught that all they see can be obtained by 'anyone' — taught, in effect, to despise the hard efforts of their parents in fields that seem too narrow, working within horizons that to their children seem like imprisonment. The result is a dependence on immigration for menial jobs, despite a relatively high level of unskilled domestic unemployment. This is unsustainable as those immigrants and their children come to aspire to more than such work too; they do not (and should not) form a permanent second class of worker drones — as of course, they are exposed to the same aspiration-machines as the other children we currently mislead in our educational system. So bringing in new workers is a one-hit, single generation plaster on the damage we have done to our society; immigration is not the answer. This disrespect for 'honest work' has been led by the middle class; beyond a traditional disdain for using one's hands, long commonplace amongst the middle, it now also has the effect of a general disinclination to work and a presumption of state management of our lives that predisposes people against undertaking strenuous efforts to improve their lot themselves.

This is true of manual jobs of real skill and pride and craftsman-ship, just as much as of more sheerly physical forms of labour. Jobs such as plumbing and carpentry go unfilled in a Britain that has shed its ancient class of artisans — whilst opportunities for outreach advisors, equality officers and health and safety inspectors bloom. The fall of metalwork and woodwork as subjects given any real cre-dence in schools combines with the generally derogatory attitude towards engineering in this country to effectively destroy our industrial creativity in a time when the world rewards few things more. In Germany or Japan, being an 'engineer' is an accolade. In Britain, our middle classes sneer at such involvement in the way things work (rather than employment in fields based on that work, where more and more in Britain are now employed). That is not merely societally unhealthy — it has also led to the loss, so surely that it would seem deliberate if one could but name those responsi-ble, of one of Britain's traditional areas of excellence.

Anti-Middle Class Bias

The middle class has largely failed to protest against the enormous anti-middle-class bias increasingly apparent in many university selection procedures: bias that seems to derive partly from the prej-udices of left-leaning dons, but is also manifested — as some selec-tors now confess — in skewed procedures that emerge as a result of pressure from government to increase the number of students from the state sector (and from various minorities within that sector). Universities such as Exeter have 'gone public' over such pressure: it has openly admitted that higher grades are required of students from private schools than from those from state schools.[30] How many more have kept quiet whilst continuing such practice? How many middle-class children are losing the university place they rightly merit? Yet the middle class remains all but silent!

This will only become worse in the future, as the Government's Higher Education Statistics Agency now publicly 'shames' those universities that are not 'inclusive enough (in 2004, 17 were listed as having 'too many' students from the independent sector).[31] We now face the prospect of funding being withdrawn from universities

[30] Simon Walters 'Sorry, if you go to a private school you'll have to get all As at A-level' p. 5 *The Mail on Sunday* 11th July 2004.

[31] John Clare 'Seventeen universities face financial penalties for failing to be 'inclusive' p. 4 *The Daily Telegraph* 30th September 2004. The universities were (in order of highest proportion of students from independent schools) Oxford, Cambridge, University College London, St Andrews, Imperial College London, Bristol, Edinburgh, the London School of

unless, in order to satisfy government quotas, they openly partici-
pate in the kind of manipulation that Exeter has admitted.

Downward Equality, University-Style

In discussing the end of the grammar school system, it was shown
that the way that's been chosen to obtain equality is to suppress
those doing well, rather than pull up those who are not. There is an
equivalent attitude looming in higher education.

Much of the destruction wrought on our educational system is
generated by resentment of the traditional educational (and social)
elite. It is ironic therefore, that whilst much elsewhere is broken, the
universities of Oxford and Cambridge largely survive in their old
form. Oxbridge is a collective last bastion of excellence. The liberal
comprehensivists are therefore sure to seek its destruction. The universities are renowned the world over for excellent teaching,
despite the lack of funds to compete with universities of compara-
ble qualities in other countries, particularly the United States: but
this counts for nothing. The elite exists, students must all be equal:
given the existence of innate ability, others cannot be raised up — so
the elite must be pulled down. The way has been shown by figures
as powerful as the current Chancellor, Gordon Brown.[32] Too late,
we will learn that 'there is one thing worse than having an elite: not
having one'.[33]

The Treatment of Students with Special Educational Needs — The Way of Things to Come

The government's current policy is to close special schools and educate special educational needs children in the mainstream.

This damages the education of both the special needs children,
and the children in mainstream education.

Economics, Exeter, Durham, King's College London, Nottingham,
Newcastle, Oxford Brookes, Leeds, Warwick, Bath.

[32] In 2000, the Chancellor labelled the decision of Magdelen College, Oxford
to reject a candidate named Laura Spence as 'absolutely scandalous', as it
was apparently based in 'old school tie' elitism against pupils from state
schools (Polly Curtis 'Woman rejected by Oxford college urges study in
the US' *The Guardian* 5th August, 2004: *http://education.guardian.co.uk/
oxbridge/article/0,5500,1276396,00.html*) — despite the fact that insufficient
places in medicine at Oxford for all top-rated candidates by A-level score (a
situation due at least in part to his government's grade inflation) and the
fact that the five successful candidates admitted instead of Laura came
from state school and minority backgrounds.

[33] *The Economist* op cit.

It is a fear of being accused of political incorrectness that prevents middle class parents — traditional complainers, instrument of propulsion in ensuring change in bad teaching practice — from objecting to this change. They fear the repercussions of pointing out the obvious: that, even putting aside the fact that the disabled child is usually no longer receiving the same quality or quantity of expert attention they require, the presence of individuals that require much more attention in a class diminishes the capacity of teaching staff to teach the other students (especially since, in a predictable progression, the falling away of the special schools has seen a reduction in the number of dedicated special needs teachers and helpers, and mainstream teachers are not nearly so well trained to cater for their needs).

No doubt there are good intentions in this scheme, though one cannot help but note that (in the short term at least, if one discounts the great costs of failing to educate someone properly) it is much cheaper. For many children, it works. But for some, it totally fails. One in five autistic children is excluded from school and never returns.[34] Many more simply lose valuable years, some neglected in classrooms, some dominating classes, most being singled out and bullied. The response amongst parents of children now so ill provided for has been text-book: in a return to the model that has driven special education since the late 1800s, parents have privately funded specialist schools for their own children and some fortunate others (an example of this is the groundbreaking work of the remarkably successful TreeHouse Trust).[35]

One would have thought that this devotion to and hard work on behalf of their children couldn't be faulted. But, unlike its response in the era of the first specialist schools, the state *frowns on* their effort rather than supporting it. In July 2004, 'parents in East Sussex who set up a special school for their autistic children were threatened with prosecution for failing to send them to a mainstream primary school'.[36] There's nothing wrong with the school concerned — it is approved by the Department for Education and Skills and passed its Ofsted inspection — it's simply that the state thinks it knows better than the parents where the relevant children belong, and will bully them to get its way.

---

[34] James Tweed and Sian Griffiths 'Building hope for autistic children' p. 13 The Sunday Times 15th August 2004.
[35] The organization has now merged with the Autism Charity PACE: *http://www.treehouse.org.uk/documents/mergerbriefing.pdf*
[36] David Harrison 'Put your autistic children into a primary school or we'll prosecute, families told' p. 10 *The Daily Telegraph* 8th August 2004.

When one lives in a nation with myriad laws designed not to stop the citizen from harming others but rather to tell the individual how to behave in arenas that for centuries have been none of the state's business, such events are quite unsurprising. The fundamental truth of parenting — that parents generally know what is best for their children — is being destroyed, but no one has really protested because the philosophy that lies behind that truth has declined. The rugged individualism and self-reliance that was once such a symbol of the middle class is systematically punished by a state that always knows best. As its tools are health and safety targets and 'standards', rather than violence and oppression, we have failed to fight it. For the most part, the instances we've seen haven't touched us yet, but eventually they will — they came for the huntsmen, but I didn't stand up for them, as I don't hunt. They came for the public schools, but I didn't stand up for them as my kids are at the comp. They came for the frightened that defend their own homes, but I didn't stand up for them, as I've not been burgled yet. They came for the parents of the disabled who tried to build schools, but I didn't stand up for them, as my children are well …

Chapter 3

The Abdication of Moral Leadership

It is fashionable to attribute the 'credit' for much of the change I have identified to an overweening media or overly aggressive commentators on society's state. But this is not right. These lobbies have simply continued to fulfil their function in a muscular, forthright way. There has always been a role for those that make questions, point out flaws. But this should, must, be a peripheral activity, one that informs the vital centre — the centre that should be 'getting on' with running things, should in essence have confidence in what we do and how we do it. But this is not the case in Britain today. Instead, the centre of attention has shifted. The best of our social commentators — comedians like Rory Bremner, playwrights like David Hare — outshine our politicians: they have not overpowered the great and the good, as much as *become* the great and the good.

Without intending to criticise the individuals concerned, this is not a healthy state of affairs: for that lobby's function, its raison d'etre, presupposes a strong establishment (of which it is not part) healthy enough to take those criticisms and continue to function. *The Goon Show* had a real, vibrant establishment to mock: whilst on reflection its poking at pomposity and hypocrisy may have played a part in starting the rot of cynicism about our political leadership, at least its sniping was from the edge, towards the vibrant, self-confident centre: not so today's *Have I Got News For You?* Satire of the centre is no longer really valid when in truth the lobby producing the satire *is* the centre. The difference between the two examples I give is that *The Goons* had a real target, which they undermined: the *HIGNFY?* team continue to plug away at a target — a functioning establishment — that no longer really exists. The commentators are predominantly a symptom, not a cause. The cause is the attitude of the politicians themselves.

The Labour government and the intellectual lobby that voted for it are more interested in, and align themselves more readily with, that satire which is traditionally the periphery and its life than with what it continues to term the 'establishment' (or, in a rare unguarded moment of revealed snarling from Mr Blair, the 'forces of conservatism'). Their arrival in power after a long period of Conservative government has seen the transfer of these doubts, these continual attacks on those that 'get on with it', from the wings, where it can do great good, to the centre, where it can only do harm. This is openly acknowledged as an aim: Hazel Blears, a minister at the Home Office, recently said that Labour 'needed to be the party of government without becoming the party of the establishment'.[1]

This facilitates the odd state of affairs in which a Party that has been in power for eight years continues to rail against 'the establishment' — when in truth they *are* the establishment. Thus a group of people has been in government for over seven years, and exercised the power of government, without ever really acknowledging that it *is* in power. It is an understandable dilemma: what does one do, having spent one's life criticising those in power, when one gains it oneself? The answer from this government and its cohorts has been to carry on criticising those now out of power as if they still had it, by way of calling them 'the establishment:' to continue to attack the largely imagined influence of the 'forces of conservatism'.

This has contributed, from the very highest level, to the downfall of authority seen across all aspects of British life. To use a currently popular catchphrase, there is a 'tipping point' in the life of society. The state can only function so long as most people respect it and its representatives, and accept its laws. Challenges to authority can only be withstood to a certain degree. When no aspect of authority receives any respect or even acknowledgment from enough people, the state breaks down. Of course, this is not in the interests of the individuals who force such crises, because the authoritarian measures needed to restore order limit their liberties as well as everyone else's — but that long-term analysis is never contemplated. At a time when the policeman is more likely to be jeered than greeted, the unwillingness of the Government to be associated with authority is bad news.

---

[1] George Jones 'Labour "could be in power for decades"' *The Daily Telegraph* 29th July 2004.

The alignment of our currently dominant political element with the 'fringe' is reflected in the bias present for so long in our public broadcasting service against the right — not necessarily in a party political way, but against the traditional values of the middle class, which is inherently conservative. It is this that Ian Curteis meant when he said in the days of Thatcher that 'in my opinion all BBC drama is now heavily biased against the Establishment and particularly against this Government.'[2] Now, these values sit at the heart of the bureaucracy: our government hates 'the establishment' — not realising that it *is* the establishment.

When our political figures were more significant in the public eye, the media paid fealty to them. Now that the situation is reversed, our political figures return the compliment. When Jeremy Paxman interviewed Ian Duncan-Smith, during his time as leader of the official Opposition in Parliament, in 2002, there was no doubting who was more powerful. The latter fawned on the former. Speaking of the campaign to keep the pound, Duncan-Smith said,

'I think that's a good idea. Don't you?'

The presenter sneered back, his disdain for his inferior openly displayed,

'Do you think I am going to walk into that?'

Duncan-Smith limply replied,

'You might. You never know.'[3]

This rather summed up not only the man but also the political world of the day — elected officials, leaders of great parties, gamely sallying forth against the media, plucky but certain to be defeated.

Jefferson rightly believed that the press was indispensable for the preservation of liberty. But his logic presupposes the need for caution against an overly dominant body politic. What should we do when the situation is reversed — when the body politic is so weak that the media has come to dominate it?

This is a change that the middle class has entirely accepted, and indeed led. Respect for leadership (and particularly for our political class), once a cornerstone middle class value, has given way to modern Britain's preference for comedians and satirists over politicians and churchmen.

---

[2] Ian Curteis 5th October 1986 quoted in *The Observer: Sayings of the Eighties* ed. Jeffrey Care (London, 1989).

[3] The transcript for this interview is available online as 'Iain Duncan-Smith Interview' at BBC Online 5th August 2002: *http://news.bbc.co.uk/1/hi/programmes/newsnight/archive/2173684.stm*

This political shift comes from an environment in which the ultimate conformity is dressed up in the clothes of non-conformity. For, overwhelmingly, attitudes held by the younger middle class are ridicule of traditional ideas, ridicule of longstanding moral norms, and an ostentatious sense of withdrawal from society. Thus modern conformity comes armed with the apparatus (and anger) of 'rebellion' and being 'outside'. This has been embraced en masse by the children of the middle class. For the first time — as they grow older, to vote, to work, to determine the direction society takes — the middle class views itself as being 'outside' the society it is subconsciously guiding.

This is exemplified by the Blair government: a government that hates convention, hates history, hates what Britain stands for, what it has been and what it is. Sometimes it is the peculiar, apparently trivial anecdote that is most revealing: 'this is the first Government in which ministers refuse flatly to be photographed near a steam locomotive or a square-rigged ship. Retrospection is a dirty word.'[4] This was not the decision of the occasional peculiar individual; rather, it was laid down by fiat: 'ministers were ordered not to not to be photographed next to buildings of any antiquity.'[5] This remains true in the second term, during which the Government has been condemned by the apolitical National Trust for consciously neglecting Britain's heritage.[6] On the part of a Government, this is unhealthy: for '... a bit of retrospection does wonders for national pride. Most of Europe knows this, and is comfortably at home with its history, folklore and country sports.'[7] Modern Britain, exemplified by its government but also more generally in its middle class, seems now to be at home with none of these things.

So government either vacillates in the face of those set on undermining traditional Britain, or actively joins in with them: where modern leadership is not characterised by weakness, it is characterised by a determination to alienate us from our past.

---

[4]   Libby Purves 'A comedy zombie movie shows what life is really like in today's Britain' *The Times* 13th April 2004.

[5]   Michael Gove 'A Scottish Historian' pp. 22–23 in 'The Brown Supremacy' *Prospect* pp. 18–28 October 2004.

[6]   Charles Clover 'Labour is failing our heritage, says trust' *The Daily Telegraph* 6th November 2004 p. 9.

[7]   Libby Purves op cit.

Changing Britain by Force:
The Blair Government and the Middle Class

'Turning the past into a foreign country'[8] is often an entirely conscious aim of our current leadership. Through the Runnymede Trust, the Blair Government established a 'Commission on the Future of Multi-Ethnic Britain' in 1998, under the chairmanship of Bhikhu Parekh. The resulting report 'can be seen as a digested expression of the transformation intended for this country'.[9]

The Parekh report considers changing Britain's name, as 'Britain' has 'systematic, largely unspoken, racial connotations... Englishness, and therefore by extension, Britishness, is racially coded'. On the contrary, one of the reasons for their enduring value as concepts is that 'Britain' and 'Britishness' are *not* exactly racially coded. Immigrants coming to this country embrace the idea of Britishness, a set of cultural values much easier to understand and an identity much easier to adopt than 'Englishness', 'Scottishness', and so forth.

Rather, this dislike of the very name of Britain reflects a hatred of our past.

Museums must be a primary target in this war against the past. They contain physical objects that real people once made and used. They help to tell us who we were and what we might be again. This is particularly so with the National Maritime Museum. That is why it has been destroyed. The new Museum removes part of this physical link. True, Nelson's uniform remains on show. But it has been removed from the full context that gave it meaning. At the centrepiece of a museum filled with guns and scale models of Dreadnaughts, it was the secular equivalent of a saint's relic. As an appendage to a politically correct circus of modern art and moans about racism and the environment, it becomes at best a piece of blue cloth with a hole in it. At worst, it becomes tainted with all the sins alleged against our country.

Do this, and opposition to the transforming of the country will be neutralised. Strip us of our national identity, and we defend our traditions and freedom with all the confidence and determination of an animal dragged from its lair.[10]

---

[8]   Sean Gabb *Cultural Revolution, Culture War: The True Battle for Britain* London, 2003 p. 22; the phrase is drawn from L.P. Hartley's *The Go-Between* (1953): 'the past is a foreign country; they do things differently there'.

[9]   Ibid. p. 23.

[10] Gabb op cit p. 25.

This change would once have been impossible, for the middle class would have forbidden it. The middle classes are the guardians of our heritage, characterised by pride in Britain and Britishness. With all its eccentricities and quirks, it once possessed a network of enthusiasts, conversationalists, amateur historians who cared about such things enough to mount campaigns, complaints, petitions — enough to convince, even when a government was peculiar enough to wish to erode its own country's sense of the past.

This might seem to paint a clichéd image of the middle class as a body of fuddy-duddy reactionaries collectively opposed to change. But one great function of the middle class *is* to be reactionary, to repeatedly offer 'a chorus of disapproval' to those that challenge the status quo: to act as a drag anchor on change, ensuring that only change worthy enough for its proponents to battle against that traditionalist framework until, grudgingly, it is accepted.

This government's ethos is not only against the tradition of the middle class ethic: that it has been allowed office with such an ethos is the *responsibility* of the middle class: bluntly, it is the fault of the middle class. For this is quintessentially a government of the middle class. After the election of Tony Blair to the leadership of the Labour Party, 'for the first time in history, Labour took a decisive lead over the Tories among middle-class voters'.[11] In the 1992 election, MORI, a polling organisation, found that the Conservative lead over Labour among ABC1 voters was 54% to 22% — more or less in line with other elections during the previous 20 years. 'In the months that followed, the gap narrowed... but it was unquestionably the advent of Mr Blair that was responsible for the breakthrough. By the late summer of 1994, ABC1s favoured Labour by 37% to 34%. From that moment, the Tories were on their way out of power.'

Whilst this government is in the vanguard of those set on the destruction of Britishness, this must not be read as being a purely party political point — both major parties have failed to preserve the proper sense of our past. This is apparent in no place more than in our schools, where the destruction of the teaching of history in any meaningful sense has ensured that our children have no real sense of where they're from or of those who came before them. Given gobbets of minutiae, normally from a piece of social history covering the plight of a supposedly downtrodden group, students gain no real sense of the span of the past in any connected way. This is a practice the Conservatives' National Curriculum made mainstream.

---

[11] 'Are they turning on Tony?' *The Economist* 13th July 2002.

More particularly, the teaching of Britain's great past is, by and large, simply abandoned, as Ofsted confirms.[12] The organisation's report on the subject showed that pupils aged from 11 to 16 receive three or four lessons on the Empire in five full school years. 'Our teenagers know all about the Nazis and trade unionism, but nothing about the Empire upon which the sun, once so famously, never set.'[13] And that information which they do receive, paints a universally negative picture of their country as an irredeemably repellent oppressor-state. As a BBC webpage designed for use in schools puts it, 'the Empire came into greatness by killing lots of people... and stealing their countries.'[14]

Our past deserves better than this. So do our forebears. The globe is spanned by nations touched by our Empire. Many have democracy, a communal commitment to liberty and the primacy of the rule of law because of it. Across those nations are the graves of many good British men and women who died building that Empire and believing in its aspirations. There should obviously be room in the study of empire and our past for the negative view. But it should certainly not be the *only* view.

Instead, the past has fallen into the hands of those that were once on the fringe of study because they chipped away and chipped away at the certainties that held up our sense of what our history is. Now in control, the history they teach is the all-but meaningless social history of highly selective moments in the past, as they are unwilling to even properly enter into discussion of the rights and wrongs of the central events of Britain's history. But an understanding of the past is so vital to understanding our country and the world now that without it our children are remarkably ignorant about their environment.

That ignorance is not merely about events, but also extends to our failure to instil a sense of how to behave, or exert moral judgment:

> We have abandoned the task of teaching our children a clear sense of right and wrong because we are not sure there is such a thing, and, when they need us, we are not there. We have given our children videos but not our time. We have given them condoms, but not a sense of self-restraint. Who can blame them if they translate the rela-

---

[12] Andrew Cunningham 'How teachers killed off our heroes' p. 21 *The Daily Telegraph* 14th July 2004.

[13] Ibid.

[14] Ibid.

tivities of our ethics into the proposition that what is right is what I feel like and can get away with?[15]

I have enlarged upon this further in relation to the family and to education. But it is helpful to point to this lack of leadership here. For from the highest politics in the country to the teaching carried out in the smallest classroom, we have allowed the fringe to capture the castle. We experience leadership without leading.

When It Does Lead, It Leads With Hate

Alone amongst the nations of the world, Britain's intellectual set hates its country.

They look down on the common tastes and vulgarities of the working class, revile the attitudes and lives of the aristocracy, and most of all, sneer at and despise the quiet solidity and dependability of the middle class. They exhibit a peculiar sense of dislocation from the society around them. They seem to believe they occupy a curious position, in Britain yet not of it. In their streets, at their work, around their dinner tables, everyone they know thinks the same things as them. A groupthink develops. When elections favour their party it is because of their inescapable rightness, and when elections go against them it is because of the electorate's stupidity. Perhaps 'twere ever thus. But this group is now particularly influential on the political and media worlds.

They actively seek the narrowing of the political exchange, by making words and attitudes so unpopular and unwelcome that they might as well have been censored. Those voicing them — the fox-hunters, the pro-lifers, the conservative, the religious — are ridiculed and castigated to the point that they approach the public sphere — if at all — cap in hand, afraid to speak up, knowing the torrent of sneering abuse that will follow.

During a recent debate at the Durham Union in which I took part, another speaker began his speech with the words 'I want to talk about morality' — and was hissed. For in Britain, people shy away completely even from mentioning that there might be such a thing as a moral code, as right and wrong, unless it is to regurgitate the currently fashionable liberal mantra. It seems that there is no value system one can publicly admit to owning. Speaking of one's morals or morality in modern Britain, other than to parrot the latest line in

---

[15] Jonathan Sachs, quoted in John Patten *Things to Come: The Tories in the 21st Century* (London, 1995) pp. 38–39.

anything-goes thinking, is treated as if it's akin to boasting of abusing children.

In the post-1997 era, this is true across the political spectrum, as the Conservative response to its failure to live up to its moral agenda, in the 'back to basics' episode and the scarring crises of personal sleaze in government, has been to conclude that it's safest not to *have* a moral agenda:

> The new Conservative leader William Hague raised eyebrows when, at his 1997 party conference, he endorsed Michael Portillo's new-found enthusiasm for non-judgmentalism in family life. Suddenly, the traditional family found itself deserted. No one in public life seemed prepared to acknowledge that intact, stable families could only be supported by preferring and according privilege to marriage over un-marriage. Instead of choosing which side of the chasm on which to stand, public figures seemed to believe that tolerance now required an abdication of moral judgment.[16]

This is an absurd reduction of moral perspective, from something that exists in and of itself to something that merely serves to facilitate easier or better relationships with others. Their defining belief is about the relationship of their attitudes with the beliefs of others. What virtue is there to tolerance, if one believes in nothing but being tolerant in the first place?

The politicians of our age have, uniquely, decided not to play a part in helping to form the societal consensus on how and how not to behave. There are two potential motivations for doing so.

The first is that they don't believe that they should attempt to influence the way others lead their lives — in which case, as society's leaders, they are abdicating from one of their key roles.

The second possibility, which one finds more likely, is that they wish to avoid the charge of hypocrisy if and when they or their party colleagues transgress against the values that have been espoused. Beyond being obviously unpleasantly self-centred (politicians do their jobs to serve the public, not to ensure they can continue to keep their jobs), this means that an entire tranche of political life has been — by common party consensus — written out of the work and thought of politicians for a calculating and pretty marginal reason, which is faulty anyway since it is absurd to suggest that just because politicians have failed to give leadership on moral issues, they are unaware of boundaries and transgressions. David Blunkett said almost nothing about family life and marriage in his political career — this does not mean that, had he offered that as a

---

[16]   Melanie Phillips *All Must Have Prizes* (London 1997, revised ed) p. xix.

defence, we might credibly have thought that he didn't know it was wrong to sleep with another man's wife.

Furthermore, the fact that that a number of Conservative politicians breached the moral standards advocated by the Government in which they served meant that they'd personally failed to live up to rules that were nevertheless correct, not that the rules should be abandoned. Individuals sometimes fail. The system shouldn't be changed to facilitate the lowest common denominator of moral failure, or abandoned altogether, because of it.

This abdication from judgment is seen across the societal board, but the result of the effective collapse of British morals is evidenced most clearly in the diminishing role the family plays in shaping both individuals and our public life.

Failing the Family

One of the greatest threats we face in the new century is not some particularly vicious economic manifestation of Disraeli's two nations. Rather, it is likely to appear from the deep division between those who have enjoyed and benefited from a stable and caring upbringing in their families, and those who have not.[17]

Individuals are entitled to take a moral position on the lifestyles of others. More than entitled — often, they *should*. It seems peculiar to have to state this, but in the modern 'hands-off' environment it seems necessary. This fact is especially true with regard to the raising of children, an area in which a wealth of knowledge exists, but is increasingly ignored.

There are age-old wisdoms, traditionally held in common, about the benefit of an example being set by parents in their behaviour, and the best methods to use. Ours is the first age to consciously discard that kitty of knowledge in favour of sloganeering and 'empowerment' that acts to cover up the fact that, by and large, modern parenthood is patently failing. In its arrogance, the current generation presumes that all that is new is best, and the slice of mankind currently alive knows more than all that have ever preceded it.

The growing trend towards sympathy for one-parent families (in itself, not necessarily a fault), complemented by aggressive attacks on those who attempt to promote the benefits of marriage as being (at best) 'old-fashioned', has overbalanced the social environment, to a position in which the silence on the issue seems to imply that no

---

[17] John Patten *Things to Come: The Tories in the 21st Century* London, 1995 p. 137.

situation is better than another. Similarly, the phenomenon of 'rotating parenting' is increasingly commonplace, as serial monogamists change partners again and again — this, too, goes unchallenged.

This is wrong. There is no moral equality between raising children inside and outside marriage. There is no moral equality between one or both parents raising children. Children are raised best in families with both parents present and married. Every possible criterion — health, educational success, chances of becoming involved in criminal activity, everything — shows that.

The Office for National Statistics reports that in 2003, 153,490 couples divorced. Half of those couples had at least one child below the age of 16, and a fifth had children under the age of five.[18]

Thus, just as 'the family is a social good',[19] so divorce is a social ill. In the modern climate of sympathy, it seems we must never condemn those who allow their marriage to fail. This is peculiar, given the mawkish sentimentality towards children that is otherwise omnipresent in the interpretation of events prevalent in today's climate.

The splintering of families is also one of the driving forces in the trend of home building, as more and more families are broken up into groups or individuals living separately. This is a serious issue, since Britain is already the most urbanised country in Europe.[20] The homeless organisation 'Crisis' agreed with a recent government report which revealed that divorce and relationship breakdown has created an unprecedented number of homeless people, particularly in the over-50s bracket; Crisis reports that 53% of those that lose their home do so after splitting with a partner. Another organisation for the homeless, 'Shelter', puts the figure for former householders now homeless as a direct result of relationship breakdown at 27,000 a year — and rising.[21]

For these reasons we should openly disapprove of divorce.

As with many issues this book touches upon, such as finance or crime, the state is not helping the situation. Here, this is manifested in the unwillingness of the state to make the process of divorce more difficult, or to apportion blame in divorce in the aftermath of the

---

[18] Sarah Womack 'Marriage is only till 30 do us part' p. 1 *The Daily Telegraph* 1st September 2004.

[19] Patten p. 139.

[20] John Reader and Sheila Dillon 'Harvest in the City' pp. 24–25 *The Times* 28th August 2004.

[21] All figures from Sarah Womack 'More over-50s homeless due to rise in divorce' p. 10 *The Daily Telegraph* 30th August 2004.

Divorce Reform Act 1969 — a situation that allows the adulterer in a relationship to divorce a blameless partner and still gain a house they contributed little to in the settlement. The state can certainly do better. However, as in the example of crime, it is predominantly down to individuals to make society change, by exercising their influence over their fellow citizens to induce feelings in transgressors that might restore proper moral norms: in short, shame is good. It was apt that 2004's breakthrough TV show was called 'Shameless'. Because that's what modern Britain is. The very concept of shame now has little or no meaning to the majority of Britons. The moral import of something being 'shameful' has been entirely lost.

It is almost impossible to overstate the extent to which we listen to those around us in framing the way we see ourselves, and in judging not just the self-interested wisdom of, but also the morality of, decisions we make in our lives. It's almost impossible to overstate how much the judgments of others matter to us as individuals, even to those of us who profess not to care a jot. It seems perfectly sensible to speculate that if, when one was contemplating separation, a friend said to one, 'don't do it — you should try harder', one might think again. If we lived in a society where condemnation of divorce was widespread, and we knew that *many* would view us poorly for that choice, we certainly would.

It is true that this morality is oppressive. It would keep some people in relationships they resent and want to get out of. But social mores are blunt tools, tools that are never wielded without *some* cost to *somebody*. Once individuals voluntarily assume the great responsibility of marriage and parenthood (decisions that ought to be carefully and realistically considered, never taken lightly), they should try extremely hard — and be made by the weight of social opprobrium to try extremely hard — to make that marriage work and keep that family together. We have undermined our ability to encourage people to do the right thing, by removing the stigma from doing the wrong thing. Of course, there are many pressures on marriage in modern society, not least the commonly held belief that one should indulge in whatever appeals and sates in the short term (such as adultery) — 'if it feels good, do it!'[22] — rather than adhering to 'old-fashioned' morality and taking a view of what is best for the long term (such as fidelity). Nevertheless, the total lack of shame

---

[22] US Senator Rick Santorum points to the widespread adherence to the 1960s philosophy: 'if it feels good, do it!' in 'The Necessity of Marriage', a speech given on 20th October 2003:
http://www.heritage.org/Research/Family/HL-804.cfm

associated with divorce is not without significance. In fostering a laissez faire societal attitude to marriage, the often marginal short-term happiness (or relief) of some individuals has come to outweigh the basic long-term interests of society — that cannot be right.

Parents look after their children better than anyone else because they care more than anyone else. They should be encouraged to do so by those around them, and by the state. The state can aid individuals to maintain beneficial parent-child relationships by fiscally empowering them to remain at home rather than forcing them to work in order to survive. Once, it did. Now, our tax system is 'not merely family neutral — it is actually biased towards those parents who work outside the home and employ other people to care for their children'.[23]

We have accepted the semi-fiction of 'quality time', a concept invented at least in part to conceal the lack of *quantity* time we spend together as families. The time parents spend time with their children ought, of course, to be more than merely mechanical, more than the mere presence of adults and children in the same place at the same time. But quantity is hugely important, and the idea of 'quality' time is a plaster applied to the increasingly small amount of time we devote to our children.

This trend is not merely driven by changes in individual attitudes. It is also propelled by tax incentives that push women back to work rather than ensuring that it is financially viable for them to remain at home if they wish to. A supposedly empowering feminist agenda demands this — as childcare 'liberates' women from the home and allows them to get back to work — and criticism of it is stifled by the stigma of the accusation of sexism. Even if one accepts the aim that both parents should be urged to go back to work, which I do not, this is actually rather old fashioned: it sees only two options, 'working mother' or 'stay at home mother', where actually there are many, as the success of flexitime arrangements through such websites as www.flexecutive.co.uk demonstrates: job-sharing can allow mothers and fathers to have a productive, fulfilling career *and* spend proper time with their children. As proponents of flexitime point out, job-sharing arrangements akin to flexitime have taken place in high-profile professions for some time: 'on a long-haul flight, passengers do not know when one pilot hands control to the other... and over a 24-hour period a patient receives care

[23] Melanie McDonagh 'Both left and right are letting the family vote go begging' p. 17 *The Sunday Times* 15th August 2004.

from many different people.'[24] Rather than encouraging such initiatives to facilitate more time with children for parents, the Government continue to push for both parents to return to full-time work as soon as possible. As a corollary to his plan for schools to remain open for longer, Charles Clarke suggests that nurseries should stay open for twelve hours a day, to facilitate even greater use of them by working mothers. The Government continues to increase provision for nursery places for babies, despite research that shows that children under the age of two benefit even more than older children from being cared for at home.

In the battle for sexual equality, for political reasons childcare conducted by people other than a child's parents has been portrayed as an unblemished good. It is time, in what one hopes is the post-feminist age, to recognise its shortcomings, which are felt most of all by the children that experience it. Of course, it is best for a child to have both parents regularly caring for it. But one is better than none, and given the realities of the necessity to earn, often the best that can be hoped for. Direct care should be encouraged, not discouraged — for parenthood cannot be outsourced.

Generational Isolation

The cost of being effectively cut off from parental and familial influence is great. The current young generation seems to me to be more lost, more separated from the rest of society, than any before it. Children gain more from contact with their peers than from parents and adults more generally. This is not merely a society that experiences a divide between grown ups and children: it also reflects a culture that is lonelier. 60% of 11–14 year olds have no strong sense of family. Over half prefer to spend time on their own. A third never play with other children.[25] 79% of all children have their own television. Shockingly, the majority of children under *five* have a TV in their bedrooms.[26]

Unsurprisingly, this means that parents have given up control over both how much television children watch, and what content that viewing takes (or perhaps, relieved at the arrival of this glowing pseudo-childminder, parents simply don't care what's

---

[24] Margarette Driscoll 'Superwoman yields to flexi-girl in the office' p. 5 News Review *The Sunday Times* DATE???

[25] India Knight 'Keeping up with the chavs' p. 4 News Review *The Sunday Times* 15th August 2004.

[26] Virgin Money 'Parents splash out £6.3 Billion to give kids "designer dens"': *http://uk.virginmoney.com/Images/designer-dens%20-consumer_tcm10-7955.doc*

watched: 68% of children say that they are not forbidden to watch any programme). About half of all children (47% of those at primary schools and 50% of those at secondary schools) watch more than 4 hours of television a day. Programmes with graphic violence and sexual content are not only viewed, but also often preferred.[27]

It is obvious that children are going to be affected in *some* way by this. If there is an argument that the effect will be positive in nature, what is it?

Even if there is such an argument, the actions of today's parents haven't been taken with it in mind. For it's not as if parents have consciously decided that this constant exposure to adult imagery and themes is good for their children. Rather, this trend is the result of a combination of benign neglect, being 'too busy' to properly supervise, and being unable to stand up to one's own offspring, who demand unrestrained access to TV.

The messages children learn from this medium gain in power because they're not offset by positive moral lessons imparted by families.

When children *do* come to learn lessons from people in their lives, they are more likely to learn from their peers than from anyone else. The teaching of adults is generally rejected, as if age is a bar on knowledge or understanding, per se. Educational interaction in society seems more horizontal — intragenerational — than vertical — intergenerational. The logical way to remedy this — to compel more of some types of contact, and limit others — simply seems beyond most parents, who are totally unable to control their children.

Perhaps every new generation seems to exhibit this rudderlessness to the older. But I believe that the 'tension created by the skewered relationship between the values of our fathers and the world of our sons'[28] is stronger than ever: the generational gap between those in their 20s today and their parents is near unique because the senior generation has decided not to fill its steadying role, in which 'values cascade from one generation to the next'[29] — instead, that generation has preferred to indulge itself into its thirties and forties. That older generation chose not to grow up; by failing to set the example of adulthood, they denied it to the generation that followed.

[27]   Chris Hastings, Julie Henry and Iwan Price-Evans 'Children "watch more than 4 hours of TV a day"' p. 9 *The Sunday Telegraph* 25th July 2004.

[28]   John Morton Blum *The Republican Roosevelt* (Cambridge, MA 1977) p. x.

[29]   Patten op cit p. 138.

This is exacerbated by the speed of post-war cultural change, which has left the generation that fought the war totally unable to understand today's young people. The new generation are unable to understand or comprehend an environment of rigid organisations and structures, that of the old world; the old generation is incapable of understanding this new generation, lost Britains that are ageing utterly without guidance — getting older, but not growing up. The generation in between, that could explain each to the other, has abdicated its responsibility.

Discipline

Mine is a self-indulgent generation. We behave like this because we have been taught to by our parents, the generation of the 1960s. Without guidance, my generation didn't grow up in the traditions and patterns that have characterised Britain for so many years — thus in two generations age-old wisdoms have been discarded, wholesale. This displays just how important the family is in determining how society works.

The family is or should be a miniature social contract, in which parents provide for the needs of their children, and in return the child accepts the discipline imposed by them. Instead, modern parents have often allowed themselves to get into a position in which they fulfil their side of the contract, and the children fulfil no element of theirs. Children even manifest outrage when their parents enquire into where they spend their time, or who with, or — heaven forbid — attempt to restrict any element of such things. Their world lacks discipline even to the point when such emotions are not feigned, but real.

How can it plausibly be suggested that this does not explain, at least in part, the behaviour of the teenagers these children will become when they grow up? Older by five years and more, their counterparts habitually vomit in the streets, having deliberately consumed more alcohol than they could possibly keep down. They exhibit a near-total absence of manners, the most obvious element of which being the fact that swearing is an absolutely standard part of their vocabulary. They are far more violent than their forbears. This behaviour is — hopefully — deplored by the parents of those that are destined to become them in the near future. Why don't those parents see a connection?

One might have thought that as the child's commitment to his side of the bargain declined, so the parent's would too. In fact, parental sacrifice has only *grown* in the face of the obsession of youth with itself, as parents give money they can often ill-afford for expensive trainers, mobile telephones and designer clothes, sacrificing their own pleasure and financial security in a way their more disciplinarian predecessors would find little other than bizarre.

Indeed, the 'disciplinarian' aspect of parenthood is all-important in this discussion. For, whilst parents pump ever more of their money, time and energy into the unfillable engine of demand that is their child, they do not engage in any serious effort towards disciplining them. Petulance is our national pre-pubescent characteristic (it mingles with aggression in the teenage years). Faced with this, instead of attempting to bring up mature adults-to-be, parents offer no discipline and deny nothing. This is absolutely not in the best interests of children: indeed, it is an abrogation of responsibility, ignoring the most basic of time-honoured facts — that adults often know better than children what is good for them. There are many rules that children dislike that need to be imposed, and many things that children want that they should be denied.

This indulgence spreads its effects into middle age. Our middle class indulges itself in an extended childhood — we take longer to marry, longer to buy property, spend more time in full-time education (in which more and more debt is incurred). This is not the case with our generally industrious immigrant middle class — who are thriving, hardworking, and sport solid commitments to the family and to conservative moral values.

Naturally in today's uber-liberal environment, one of the most important aspects of appropriate denial is the most ridiculed. The middle class seems to have entirely given up on any suggestion that children should be led away from having intercourse early — instead, children having sex is sees as entirely inevitable, an unavoidable and uncontrollable pitfall of modern life. This fallacious concept has permeated British society to the extent that it appears as truism even in traditionally conservative powerhouses such as *The Daily Telegraph*, which recently summed up the 'members of the abstinence club' as being 'the terminally shy, the facially challenged and the trainspotting community'[30] — a damaging suggestion that carries with it the implicit idea that the total lack of sexual mores amongst young Britons is somehow laudable.

Of course, it is not. The Health Protection Agency's report shows that between 1995 and 2003 the number of Chlamydia cases rose by

---

[30] 'Sex please, we're human' *The Daily Telegraph* 13th July 2004.

192%, syphilis by an astounding 1,058% and gonorrhoea 139%.[31] One in eight girls aged 16-19 has Chlamydia, and one in five aged 16-18 has used the morning after pill.[32] The response from the Government and the British Medical Association (which at least admits that there is a crisis[33]) is to aim for more efficiency in treatment in sexual health clinics. The environment that facilitates the behaviour that leads to such infection apparently goes unquestioned.

Much of this environment results from the government's programme of free contraception for teens (including the morning after pill), which has the exact opposite effect to that which is intended. Nottingham University's recent report has shown that the programme boosts venereal disease, and — obviously, given that it tacitly condones the act — encourages teen promiscuity.[34] The report's statistical analysis showed that both teen sexual activity and sexually transmitted diseases amongst teens have increased fastest in the areas that implemented the Government's policies most fully.

The second important cause of the current atmosphere of unquestioned sexual liberalism amongst the young is the programme of sex education practised in British schools, which achieves precisely the ends it supposedly aspires to prevent. It is universally conducted in our schools largely without complaint from the middle class or anyone else. We are always told that one of the reasons that middle class children apparently receive better education is that their parents care enough to be involved — to be busybodies in the school's practice. On the contrary, this is not happening, and should: the ever-growing practice of sex education demonstrates this, because if parents really did intervene to ensure the best interests of their children, schools would be besieged because of these lessons and the ill effects they engender.

Sex education leads to experimentation and early intercourse, and indirectly encourages promiscuity. The *most* moral form of sex education says 'you shouldn't do this, but we know you are': thus pushing children to consider their sexual existence before they need to or indeed should. In this way, sex education's message is invariably confused — on the one hand, by saying 'here are the perils of teen sex, so don't do it', and on the other hand, 'here is how to have

[31] Celia Hall 'Sexual disease epidemic threatens Britain's young' p. 6 *The Daily Telegraph* 28th July 2004.

[32] Jenny Hope 'The Sexual Epidemic' p. 4 *The Daily Mail* 30th September 2004.

[33] Hall op cit.

[34] Alexandra Frean 'Free contraception "boosts teen promiscuity and VD"' p. 1 *The Times* 5th April 2004.

teen sex safely'. Less moral forms start by saying, 'the best form of a relationship is a loving, constant relationship' and then says, here are the ways to use protection if you're *not* in such a relationship' — a logic which doesn't even attempt to suggest that children should not be sexually active, and *presumes* that the members of the class are in sexual relationships already.

The justification for this is that 'adolescents know all about sex' — an idea pushed in our permissive society so much it's almost a truism. Contrary to that bland generalisation, even in Britain today, many children *don't* have sex early, and don't think about such things — they actually have childhoods. For such children, these lessons stir up confusion, misplaced embarrassment or even shame at perfectly natural slower development. Week in, week out, we are pushing such children from childhood into a sexualised existence: and the middle class, traditionally society's leading light in determining morality in our schools, does nothing about it.

Lessons also encourage children to view their peers in a sexualised context. The openness with which sex education tells students to treat sex encourages them to ask one another the most personal questions ('have you lost your virginity?': how embarrassing, how uncool, to have to say no), and to transgress personal boundaries — all with the teacher's approval. Inhibitions are broken down not just by peer pressure, but also by the classroom. Week in, week out, the state is actively victimising in the classroom children who want to say 'no': and the middle class does nothing about it.

Sex education informs children about sex, and then invites them to make a choice. But as demonstrated all the time, children are bad decision-makers, often choosing what is bad for them. That is why adult society often needs to decide for them — what they should eat, what they should watch on TV, when they are mature enough to be able to choose whether or not to drink or smoke. Sex is just as important as those things — just as dangerous, and just as potentially destructive. The abdication of our responsibility in the sexual arena is shameful. We should be unafraid to tell children this is something they cannot do, aren't mature enough to consent to yet — a responsibility we shrink from even though it is reflected by the stated aim of society enshrined in the law of the age of consent. Lessons implicitly lauding the pleasures of intercourse are entirely contrary to that aim.

Furthermore, why do we entrust 'sex education' to the state in the first place? Teaching this subject en masse in a classroom reduces it to biological notions, group embarrassment and crude jokes. Children have never needed this from the state: left alone, they learn from their family and surroundings and grow naturally into adults without the state's involvement. Few things are responsible for parental disaffection with education more than the teaching of sex and sexuality in ways contrary to their wishes. Parents have a right to determine the moral environment in which their children develop and this is a huge intrusion into that right.

That moral environment has been manipulated again and again over the last fifty years by a liberal teaching establishment set on undermining traditional values and beliefs. Sex education has been a prime weapon in that social engineering. That tool should be taken away from teachers, who as a body have proven themselves undeserving of it. It has been proven again and again that 'sex education' in this country occurs without any reference to moral values. As for the tedious idea that children somehow need the nanny state to look after their sexuality: who knows children and their needs better than parents and families? Schools are responsible for so much that is wrong with our children, and by giving them free licence to delve into students' sexuality, things become so much worse, blurring the line between teacher, adviser, confidante, and sometimes in extremes, between teacher and lover — an abuse of power that bringing sex into the classroom makes so much easier. It is not only the case that mature, sensitive instruction in sex and the issues surrounding it is made impossible by being part of the state curriculum. Conversely, the role of the classroom as a place of instruction is undermined by sex education. In one lesson, children are given condoms to put on bananas – in the next, asked to concentrate in a disciplined fashion on literature or maths. Understandably, that doesn't occur — the classroom has become a place of crudity and sexualised observation, rather than a place carrying out its purpose — of instructing children in a way enabling them to learn. This requires a certain seriousness and clarity of purpose that sex education destroys.

Children have a well known, innate desire to do the forbidden. Once intercourse becomes a mainstream discussion, a situation sex education facilitates, adolescents enter into ever more extreme activities in order to still maintain that thrill of transgression – anal sex, group sex, sado-masochistic activity.

Sex education classes for those under the age of consent tacitly approves of breaking the law. It says, 'don't do this — but given that you *are*, do this, this and this'. This sends a terrible message about the law — that breaking it isn't serious, that authority (as represented by teachers) tacitly approves of that illegality, will tolerate it and even encourage it. Sex education fails to sufficiently tell our children what is right and what is wrong. Then it says, this is supposedly wrong — but nudge nudge, wink wink ...

Very few teachers want to teach this subject, so the quality of teaching is generally awful. Those that do end up teaching it are often the oddest characters in the teaching establishment. Many teachers happy to 'cover' other subjects are uniquely embarrassed by this one and will not do so.

Finally, sex education serves well as a symbol of the changed position of the individual in modern Britain. If on the one hand our children are ignorant about sex and sexuality, then they shouldn't be taught about it and won't enter into it until ready. If on the other hand, as pro-sex education advocates maintain, they know all about it and do it anyway, then they shouldn't be mollycoddled by the state. They should take responsibility for their own actions. We live in an indulgence culture, where nothing is ever anyone's fault. This is wrong, and we should be unafraid to say to individuals that they must live up to the consequences of choices they make. If teenagers get pregnant or get another teenager pregnant, that is *their fault* and they should live with the results. We shouldn't set out to ruin our educational system to pander to such behaviour. Indeed, if we stopped *sympathising* quite so much and *judged* a little more, perhaps fewer teens would be rushing to copulate.

Even on its own terms, the teaching of this 'lesson' has failed. Its traditional justification is that it can combat ignorance. Given the STD rates cited and the fact that Britain's teen pregnancy rate is one of the highest in the developed world *with* over 50 years of sex education classes, they can hardly be declared to have been a success in combating this: 50 years ago, the argument for introducing sex education was ignorance amongst children. 50 years later, the argument for retaining sex education is ... ignorance amongst children.

The whole of the broader liberal approach to sexuality in Britain has failed. 'Expanding contraceptive services and providing the morning-after pill free to teenagers have encouraged sexual behaviour rather than reduced it.'[35] As Robert Whelan of Civitas points out, this has become apparent despite the fact that 'by making the morning-after pill free to teenagers, the Government had masked real levels of sexual activity ... [As,] because the pill causes early abortions, some conceptions were not counted in teenage preg-

---

[35] Alexandra Frean op cit quoting from the Nottingham University report.

nancy figures.' The report also found that the government's liberal contraception policy has had 'an adverse impact on sexually transmitted infections.'

The experiment with liberalism should be stopped. Obviously, it has had a corrosive effect on public morality — but the facts and figures show that it has failed even on its own terms.

Chapter 4

The Route of the Abdication: Government Policy

... they are well aware of human suffering but refuse to take it seriously.
They take the lives of men to be as frivolous as their own, they meddle with
the former for fun, and then get bored.

W.H. Auden[1]

This chapter illustrates the betrayal of middle class values at every
level of Government across a wide range of policies. Policies of governments of both hues have resulted (often deliberately) in the
diminishment of individual freedom and the undermining of middle class values, especially when accompanied by a conscious rejection of those values by at least some in society.

Government's role in the 'broken windows for morality' theory I
am propounding must necessarily be limited, as the very point of it
is that individuals do it themselves, *want* to do it themselves, rather
than being compelled to act in certain ways by the state; 'the importance of customs, traditions and moral values as a means of regulat-
ing behaviour is that people behave themselves even if nobody's
watching.'[2] Moral opprobrium must be imposed by individuals
because if their attitude is merely parroted in response to government, once the eye of the state is off the citizen then they won't
behave like that any more. When individuals reject the values that
glue society together, if that society is to remain free the responsibil-

[1] *The Dyer's Hand & Other Essays* (London, 1963) p. 429. For the sake of
     honesty it should be stated that Auden is referring to Homeric gods, not
     post-war British politicians — though the similarities are remarkable.
[2] Walter E Williams 'Attack on Decency' 1st December 2004:
     http://www.townhall.com/columnists/walterwilliams/ww20041201.shtml

ity to punish those individuals rests not with government but with other individuals — through condemnation, castigation and shame, as discussed previously.

However, whilst its positive capacity is therefore limited, government does have 'the power to harm'. When it wields it, it can — and does — undermine beneficial cultural values. This is especially true when its power is used in tandem with concomitant efforts towards that end by individuals.

Finance

In the opening chapter, I posited the theory that the middle class work ethic has changed. Once, individuals within the middle class distinguished themselves from the working class by their willingness to support themselves, and having the liberty to determine their future, by virtue of their hard work. Now on the other hand, there is a far greater reliance on the state — both for money to fund living, and for guidance on how to conduct that life. This middle class adoption of a dependency outlook traditionally only seen amongst the working class is troubling. The difference is that the working class traditionally *has* to depend on another's leadership due to practical (financial) circumstances — a logical thing to do — whilst for the middle class, this reliance is a voluntarily limitation on its imagination and self-reliance even though its members are financially and materially capable of deciding their future for themselves. Our working class has had to yield to the state, as it was in its best interests. Our middle class has *of its own volition* surrendered to the wise, all-knowing state rather than living with the frets of independence involved in governing its fate itself.

In return, if the middle class gets the occasional apparent break around election time it counts itself lucky. But it doesn't consider where the break comes from. We are allowing ourselves to be bribed with our own money.

The state is encouraging this culture of dependence. It does so through excessive taxation, which puts the individual at the mercy of government rather than allowing him control of his own future. Of course, taxation at this extreme level is a comparatively recent trend in British social behaviour: taxation is hardly a new thing — it is a question of degree.

Recent figures released by the accountants Smith and Williamson[3] have revealed that those earning £40,000 lose as much as half of that money to the treasury, through direct and indirect taxation. The government disputed this, a treasury spokesman saying that it is 'notoriously difficult to measure the burden of indirect taxation' — which presumably explains its appeal to government.

If a man earns £40,000 and can spend it as he wishes, he is his own master. If he is taxed £4,000 of it, he has contributed to the infrastructure that makes social living viable but is still able to govern his future. But tax him — directly and indirectly — £12,000, £15,000 or even more, and control passes to the state to give some of that money back or not, at its whim — in benefits for the bringing up of children, in provision for cheaper public transport on which the individual is now reliant as they cannot afford their own, in various subsidies. The individual is often grateful to the state for that provision, as otherwise all those things would present real stumbling blocks in his life — but the situation is possible only because the state took his money from him in the first place.

The result is a middle class that thinks less and less about deciding its own destiny, and providing for its future, as it seems government guarantees it will take care of such things — a promise no government can ever live up to, a pledge that will only ever result in disappointment. Increasingly, the young middle class is giving up its ability to use initiative and entrepreneurial skills to decide its own fate, prolonging its time in paths determined by the state by staying on at school and then by (almost automatically, without thought) going to university, and then choosing careers in the state sector, or in quasi-state employment, or choosing no employment at all.

We are taxing the middle class more than ever before. If the middle class had the chance to spend more of its own money, the result would be more significant than the saving gained in not filtering it back to them through the profligate government bureaucracy, and the benefit to the British economy in greater consumer spending (though those gains in themselves are worth having): the greatest result would be an financial re-empowerment of our middle class. There is obviously greater efficiency in the individual spending money himself rather than capital being cycled through the state's hands, given the myriad processes of collection, retention and allocation it must pass through (often with losses through inefficiency).

---

[3] Alison Steed '£40,000-a-year earners lose half to the taxman' The Daily Telegraph 4th September 2004.

Beyond this efficiency saving there is a real moral case to be made for the individual, rather than government, spending as much of his money for himself rather than government taking it to spend it for him, after provision for the real essentials of state — defence, law and order — has been made. He has earned the money — it is his to invest, to use, to donate, and to spend. This is especially true of the middle class, which has as a body always displayed a tendency towards thrift and saving rather than profligacy. We are beating the saving habit out of the middle class. When pensions are (dishonestly) taxed to the degree that they are now, why invest in pensions? When inheritance tax bites so much from the estate, why leave anything behind? The saving habit is greatly needed now: personal debt held by Britons is higher than ever before, topping a trillion pounds for the first time in 2004.[4]

This is not to say that redistributive tax is necessarily wrong. Society should indeed provide for the less well off by asking for a greater contribution from those that have more (though as the state asks for that more and more, so the most successful individuals become more inclined to leave the state, to the point that the process becomes counterproductive). That is not to say, however, that the state should assume the provision of things for individuals and families that might be provided independently instead. With regard to that kind of spending, the state's taking of capital from individuals has no moral ground, but merely a *patronising*, pragmatic one: we know best — we know better than you how to spend your money in your interests.

Whilst 'the government has a responsibility to protect the sick, the old, the unemployed, the handicapped and others in need … people should be encouraged to meet and pay the cost of many needs through contributions, rather than by simply depending on other people's money being redistributed to them'.[5] Because ever-larger numbers of people are compelled to rely on government provision of one form or another by the way the taxation system sucks capital from individuals, especially those starting out, attempting to begin lives of financial self-sufficiency, the traditional implied criticism contained in accepting hand-outs no longer really exists. But that societal disapproval can be a force for good. It encourages individuals to stand on their own feet, as they should do. Insuring oneself against future problems should be fostered, not

---

[4]   'Consumer's Trillion Pound Debt' *Prudentminds.com* 21st May 2004: *http://www.prudentminds.com/newsarticle2672791.html*

[5]   Patten p. 140.

punished with taxation on saving and effective discouragement from the universality of state handouts. Doing so is in society's interests, and in the individual's — for it forms the habit of self-reliance that is foremost in determining an individual's character.

That self-reliance is, in effect, being discouraged by the state as it attempts to grind out 'equality' despite the blindingly obvious fact that unless government totally changes the nature of society from capitalist to something else, some will always earn and have more than others. It is unfortunate that liberty and equality are posited in something as influential as the US constitution in terms that suggest they are equals. For they are not. If liberty is to exist, it must trump equality — for individuals must have the liberty to better themselves, to work and thereby acquire material for themselves and their families. Equality of *opportunity* is laudable and should be aimed at. To attempt to force equality of *status* is oppressive, deprives the individual of freedom, and destroys the incentive to work. This is good common sense, something the middle class once possessed in abundance. It seems it does not now.

Individuals are contributing to this governmental destruction of archetypal middle class value in finance — prudence, thrift — by accepting the idea that debt, if not good exactly, is at least acceptable and usual — and sometimes, for those such as students — a badge of honour. UK consumer debt is running at a record level and is getting higher every day.[6] In 2003 the total level of personal debt held by Britons stood at £156 billion,[7] and it has risen greatly since. Large numbers of individuals are habitually borrowing beyond their means. However, most don't seem to see this as a cause for concern. This is primarily because any vestige of the sense of importance one should attach to self-sufficiency, fiscal stability, to being able to 'stand on my own feet', has been given up. The idea of being in debt as a morally dubious state was an extremely useful one. That it has been lost is undoubtedly a boon for entrepreneurs, for risk-takers in business, a shift that has enabled a boom of free enterprise. But for individuals who find themselves at the mercy of banks and credit card companies, or — for the less extreme majority — in effect merely working for them for the majority of their adult lives, the fall of moral opprobrium applied to debt and of the significance

[6]   Duncan Wood 'Conspicuous Consumption' ERisk 18th October 2002: *http://www.erisk.com/ResourceCenter/Credit/ConspicuousConsumption.asp?link=*

[7]   Bank of England figures, disclosed on 'Money Box' Radio Four 1st February 2003:   *http://news.bbc.co.uk/1/shared/spl/hi/programmes/money_box/transcripts/01_02_03.txt*

attached to self-sufficiency has made their lives worse, and forces them into a subservient position vis à vis the state.

On its own, the state would have found it very difficult to undermine this value and make individuals more reliant upon it. On their own, it would have been near-impossible for individuals to achieve the demolition of thrift as a cultural virtue since the state as safety net wouldn't have picked them up, so none would have followed their example. Together, they have come a long way to achieving this end.

Inheritance Tax

The worst example of all is the state's extortionate inheritance tax (IHT). This tax is opposed to all the fiscal virtues of thrift and provision for the future that are traditionally so quintessentially middle class. Truly, with IHT, Britain's exchequer targets the most vulnerable: we are taxing the dead.

This does not encourage work; neither does it encourage saving. In this, IHT is like the scandalous tax on pensions instituted by this government — and, also like that tax, it is inflationary. Taxing in this way causes inflation because it takes saved capital and converts it into government money, which of course the government then spends.

The tax also punishes people for trying to provide for their families rather than splurging money during their own lifetime. On a societal level, we should *encourage* individuals to use the money they earn to provide for their children, not discourage it. Patrician politicians might suggest that the money is better placed in their hands, as they can guarantee the future better than individuals. This is untrue. What does the state know about provision for the next generation that the current generation does not? In saving money to give to his child, the individual is performing the most natural and laudable of parental functions — providing for his offspring after his own death. Inheritance tax deliberately attempts to exploit that desire. It is a tax on love.

It is also a tax on capital on which individuals have already been taxed. Often, this means that the state becomes the majority beneficiary of an estate. If the individual concerned was paying the higher rate of income tax during life, in paying IHT his estate has been taxed 40% on capital on which he has *already* been taxed 40%: the state takes 64% of the capital, leaving the 'inheritor' with a small 36% portion of the deceased's estate afterwards (obviously, this is often split again, when more than one person inherits).

As inflation continues to rise at a higher rate than the bands of inheritance tax are moved upwards (they are not pegged to inflation and invariably move more slowly), more and more people are made subject to this tax. The first time many individuals become subject to the higher rate of tax is on their death — naturally, many are ill-prepared for it. Many don't think they're worth the amount required, but find that the adding up of hypothetical retail value of all their possessions (a peculiar exercise few outside the Inland Revenue office ever carry out) puts them in it. The effect is significantly increased by the fact that many are pushed into the bracket by the value of their home, which has gained hugely in theoretical value since it was acquired: but no wealth has actually accrued to the people concerned unless they want to emigrate to somewhere with a very different housing market, since they still need somewhere to live.

The tax is not only wrong in principle: it is also horribly misapplied in this country, catching a higher proportion of the population than anywhere else. IHT in the UK is at 40% on everything valued over £263,000. It therefore begins at a lower rate and at a higher level than in Germany, where a 30% top rate is not applied until the estate is valued at c. £2 million. In France, the 40% top rate is applied once over £1 million.[8] This means that it catches a large chunk of the whole population, rather than a slice of the most well-off as elsewhere — and that proportion will continue to rise and rise. IHT is a convenient and dishonest way of raising more revenue for the state. Inheritance tax should be abolished altogether — as it is in Australia, New Zealand and Canada. The USA plans to phase it out by 2010. It is unjust, and deters individuals from being responsible in passing it on the capital that they have, through their endeavours, accumulated during their lives.

Capital Accumulation

Capital accumulation is a social good. The more people that can do it, the better.

Left alone, consuming what they want to consume, spending what they want to spend, individuals have greater freedom, whilst being entrusted with greater responsibility — the natural result of capitalism. We ought to accept the truths that this entails.

---

[8]   Libby Purves 'Inheritance tax hits too many people too hard — bring on some new ideas' p. 18 *The Times* 24th August 2004.

We demand a low tax, high service society. This is unobtainable. If, as seems true, we want low taxes, we must be mature in our thinking and accept its consequences. We must say to individuals that they cannot have what they believe they have a right to have. Malthus rightly distinguished the poor from undeserving poor. We cannot afford to fund the undeserving poor to the nth degree; nor should we. We should provide no IVF on the NHS, no cosmetic surgery. We should say that many 'goals' and 'targets' should be abandoned by government — this will do little harm, as for the most part, they represent the activity of government in places it never should have been in the first place.

An entire new and lifestyle has been created, at public expense — and thus draining the ability of individuals to accumulate capital, as they're being taxed to pay for it. I mean the huge mass of 'access co-ordinators', health and safety inspectors, entitlement officers, target monitors, equality facilitators, teen pregnancy advisers,[9] outreach programme administrators, five-a-day fruit-and-vegetable co- ordinators[10] ... Britannia has overseers coming out of her metaphorical ears. The government in effect gives a massive subsidy to *The Guardian* newspaper by advertising these non-jobs, in a section that often runs to over 70 pages. Such positions can be abandoned without any harm to core provision of the state's responsibilities. The effect of the individuals currently occupying them (of whom some, no doubt, are able) having to seek actually productive roles in society would have a beneficial effect on the economy, over and above the large reduction in the use of tax money their redundancy would ensure.

The middle class would once have howled in protest at the senseless ballooning of those paid from the public purse. In effect, the lives of one big chunk of the citizenry is being paid for by the efforts of another — and it's not the homeless and poverty-stricken that are receiving the money, it's the bureaucrats and administrators of the bloated state apparatus.

Those that have benefitted from the enormous post-war expansion of the bureaucratic structure (i.e. those employed in it) must justify their existence, or else be thrown out by all those that have

---

[9]   Such a post might be worthwhile if it did anything to reduce the number of teen pregnancies occurring in Britain — given their manifest failure to do so, they are as worthless as the rest of the 'jobs' on the list.

[10]   This is not facetious — the position really exists. It pays, on starting, £29K per annum. The enormous scheme's website is *http://www.5aday.nhs.uk/* and London's thirteen 5-a-day co-ordinators can be found at *http://www.5aday.nhs.uk/locally/regions/London.aspx*

suffered as a result of it (i.e. the rest of us). They know that unless they keep churning out decisions and keep ruling on things and interfering in things, people will realise that the Emperor has no clothes — that they do nothing. So they are positively motivated to keep meddling. But we are protected from the potentially ghastly full effects of this by the cruel irony that this sector is the least productive and efficient of all Britain's workers. For even if those dictums issued in the rules-for-the-sake-of-rules culture were worthwhile, they would run up against the nature of the workforce appointed to oversee them. This vast army marches into the town halls of Britain every morning, under a motto, graven in stone in letters six feet high, that stands emblazoned on the hearts and on the lips of a tranche of our for the public service: 'can't somebody else do it?'

Salisbury's Foreign Office employed 81 people. Many of London's boroughs alone employ a hundred times that number.

Government significantly effects the state's economy not merely though its controls, but also through its spending. Government creates inflation by removing capital from the private sector, frittering it in the process of collection and use, and spending it inefficiently in an environment where there is no competition. This is enhanced by government spending what it does not have, incurring high levels of debt which in turn means higher taxes in the future: citizens 'are forced to go into debt today because the ... government decided to go into debt yesterday.'[11] Huge spending drives down the value of money, prices go up, wages stay the same, and individuals become comparatively poorer.

The ability of individuals to stand on their own financial feet is central to societal strength and morale. The Government wields great power for good and for ill here. Margaret Thatcher empowered individuals by helping them to buy their own homes: she envisaged a democracy of homeowners. The current government pursues policies with results that are precisely the reverse — a combination of crippling taxation and the current housing market makes individuals much more dependent on the state. It is much harder to purchase homes, and begin lives of financial independence. Individuals who already own homes are forced to have to give up ownership of their homes in order to pay for care in their old age, or the tax levied on the death of a loved one. Recognising the benefit to society of individuals becoming homeowners — taking on responsibility, becoming grounded in a community — the Austra-

---

[11]   Richard Nixon *State of the Union Address* 22nd January 1970.

lians have a grant for first time homebuyers. In effect, we have the opposite. We are making the individual dependent on the state — the very core middle class ethic Hutber identified, fiscal independence, is being worn away.

Thus a government ostensibly shorn of ideology can now achieve what socialism failed to do: individualism is being destroyed.

Destruction of the Military

The middle class has traditionally had a huge amount invested in our armed forces.

Their children have grown up in it to be men and leaders of men. It has remained one of the last bastions of competition and vigour and unalloyed pride in both self and in country. Perhaps for these reasons, it is being torn down.

The Government recently announced a series of cuts that would reduce the number of armed forces personnel by roughly a tenth.[12] Given the level of opposition to them, these cuts may not actually occur; but they demonstrate governmental intention.

The armed forces are (just) meeting the huge demands the government is placing on them around the world. These commitments may go UP, not down, in the future. The government proposes to scrap current technology (tornadoes, jaguars) in anticipation of future technology (the typhoon, or 'Euro-fighter'). But what if the future technology doesn't come up to scratch? And what about the lag in the middle, before the new equipment is online but after the old is off?

Even more seriously, how can the government seriously propose reducing the *infantry*? Tony Blair has put our armed forces into combat more often than any Prime Minister since Churchill, who was fighting the biggest land war in history. Even if his interventionism is curbed and no further actions are taken, the level of our commitment in Iraq seems likely to go up rather than down. How can this Prime Minister in good conscience *reduce* our armed forces?

A shrinking military doesn't just lose men — it also loses history. The destruction of regiments is lamentable. It is the severing of soldiers from the deeds of their predecessors, from the glories and sacrifices of the past. The amalgamation of historic regiments into 'regiments of spin' — such as the Royal Hampshires and the Queen's Regiments becoming the mawkish Princess of Wales's

---

[12] Michael Smith and Neil Tweedie 'Cuts reduce RAF to The Few' p. 1 *The Daily Telegraph* 22nd July 2004.

Royal Regiment — destroys pride and a sense of place in traditions and achievement that serve to inspire our servicemen to deed and sacrifice for their country. The changes have, this time, been justified on the grounds of efficiency, as some regiments are now single-battalion regiments, a factor that limits their capabilities. But this is remarkably disingenuous: such regiments only *become* of single-battalion status because of previous rounds of destruction.

The reduction in infantry personnel is largely based on the improved security situation in Northern Ireland: but how do we know what will happen in the troubled province in the future?

Furthermore, we call on the army in times of national emergency, such as the Fire Brigade's strikes. One doubts that the government is in possession of an eternal assurance from the FBU that they will not strike in the future, and even if they were one wouldn't believe it. Despite the Government's dependence on the armed forces in carrying through the decisions that flow from its interventionist world view, the attack is nevertheless unsurprising, since the military is one of the few last bastions of the hated 'establishment' — a bastion of discipline, of an unashamed sense of patriotism and duty and selflessness that (lamentably) does not fit with our modern world.

General Sir Mike Jackson, shamefully put up as a political figure by the government to justify these changes (presumably as it is harder for the media to accuse him of stupidity on this topic, or of ulterior motives), said, 'It seems very improbable that Britain will have to act unilaterally in today's world.'[13]

This may be so. But it was equally improbable in 1982 when Britain went to war with Argentina after the invasion of the Falklands.

The navy has been forced to swallow a drastic, immediate reduction in its fighting capacity in return for a promise that in the future, two long-desired aircraft carriers will be bought. One truly hopes that these vessels actually arrive — but doubts that they will. Even if they do, they have been shorn of the defensive support vessels they would require.

In the past, a coalition of middle class opinion would instinctively have risen up and challenged government's desire to hack at the military structure. This seems not to happen now. It must. Beyond its own — very beneficial — historical ties to the military, the middle class should be alive to the dangers in which these 'reforms' place the state.

The accumulated kitty of our country's communal wisdom has traditionally been disproportionately vested in the middle class —

[13]   Interview, *Newsnight* 22nd July 2004.

it is from this strata of society that historians, playwrights, poets, commentators and in latter days, politicians, have tended to come. The responsibility for giving warnings and for protesting the failure to learn from past lessons falls disproportionately to the middle class, and is not being discharged. When the prudent virtue of a strong defence is forgotten, the repercussions are grievous. The last time this group collectively lost its head was in the 1930s, and the excuse of the trauma of the First World War was available. What will be said to future generations of the current lapse?

We are in the process of destroying our capability to act in our own defence. Worse than all these material cuts though, is the destruction of the *ethos* of the military. As the forces have shown from the Falklands to Iraq, even whilst grossly underequipped they possess the grit to endure and to excel. But that iron will is born of a harsh training and the teaching of a necessarily ruthless mindset, both so alien to modern British cultural mores that their anomalous position no longer seems merely strange — to some, their existence is an affront.

The military is for fighting. That's its job. To teach people to do it well, and to keep them in the shape and mindset to do it well, requires an outlook and a set of skills very different from that of civilian life. This tension has always existed, and one should not pretend that problems caused by it are new — it has always thrown up an unease with the forces that Kipling's Tommy well knew. But this 'differentness' is necessary, if the forces are to do their job.

Britain today is a much softer country than it once was. Much of the change one can observe in its history is undoubtedly good — the end of the worst forms of manual labour for instance, or of flogging. But as that trend has manifested its existence in more arguable arenas — in the removal of the power of physical chastisement from teachers and the putative removal of same from parents, for example — it makes the military's work more difficult. For tests of endurance are necessary in order to ensure that the people we put in the most grievous danger can endure *real* hardship. When this trend is combined with the modern 'rights' culture in which individuals constantly challenge and sue, the twin virtues of discipline and obedience so necessary to the military's performance become less and less automatic — even to the extent that its functionality is called into question.

It is obvious that such virtues — discipline, obedience — are the enemy of the 'free and easy' outlook dominant in British life and championed especially by the Blair government. Whilst repugnant, the position is, in general, coherent. You and I might lament their passing, but the government would not. However, in terms of the military in particular, the logic breaks down. Our rulers must now consider the paradox they have created. The values they so loathe underpin the army they like to use so much.

Health

This area, and the problems visited upon it by recent cultural change, can be dealt with very briefly.

The NHS is the second largest employer in the world, after the Indian Railway Service.[14] Despite that — despite the enormity of the funding it swallows, the staggering number of people it employs — it is undeniably in a parlous state.

There are few areas that display more directly than our hospitals the decline of authority, and of the instinctive respect for it without which it struggles to function. For without the authority of Matron, so sadly missed, the most basic things go wrong.

Consider MRSA (methicillin resistant staphylococcus aureus), known as the 'superbug'. MRSA is eminently avoidable — by simple standards of hygiene and good practice that have been in place almost since Florence Nightingale's day. Hands should be washed. Gloves should be worn. Sheets should be changed. Floors should be scrubbed. Bedpans should be emptied. This is not the stuff of genius, or of high technology. Indeed, it's perfected in many countries much, much poorer than Britain.

But, despite all the attention given to the problem following recent publicity, the rate of NHS patients dying from the bug is on the increase. Officially, 7,600 people die of MRSA in the blood every year in NHS hospitals. The actual rate may be much higher, since individuals may die of MRSA but a post-mortem is not performed and death is ascribed to some other cause. But that's the official rate. Compare it with the rate in private hospitals: BMI Healthcare, the largest private healthcare group in the UK, has 47 hospitals and treats a million patients a year.

Their rate of death every year: zero. In fact, their rate of infection in the blood: zero. There has *never* been a case of MRSA in the blood in a BMI Healthcare hospital.[15] Of course, it is true that such hospi-

---

[14] 'Right Data, Right Place, Right Time — Joined Up Medical Records?' *The European Information Society Group January* 2003: *http://www.eurim.org/briefings/statusr/SharingDatasr.htm*

[15] James Bartholomew 'Private hospitals don't get MRSA' *The Sunday Telegraph* 25th July 2004.

tals handle nothing like the number of in-patients (most likely to contract MRSA) as the NHS. But not to have had a single case is remarkable.

It is undoubtedly the case that there are other reasons for the depressingly low morale of the health service. Nursing is a vocation. People go into it despite the bad pay and terrible conditions. We should reward those that choose it, and encourage those considering it to do so, by improving both. We should also try to wean ourselves off our undesirable reliance on agency staff. Moreover though, a proper system of authority must be re-established, in which basic standards of cleanliness are rigidly enforced. If this entails re-recruiting the 50-something generation of former nurses to show their replacements how it's done, then that is what we should do.

Different Aspects of the Same Problem

The decline of respect for authority figures has occurred over several decades, in the post-war period. It happened steadily. Its existence was hardly a secret — those that championed it did so openly, brazenly — they were and are proud of their struggle and eventual triumph. The innate respect for authority the middle class once held as the bedrock of its approach to societal interaction has been chipped away. All the institutions of Britain and Britishness — the military, the health service, the police force — have seen it and suffered from it. Restoring that respect is a Herculean task and it falls to the middle class, who have allowed it to erode. It can be done, by many working together. Whether the will exists is another question.

Chapter 5

The Abdication of Cultural Identity

It is unsurprising that much of the racial tension experienced in this country occurs amongst the poorest communities. In today's society, 'one in five believes that immigrants should get less welfare support than existing British citizens ... views differ most according to social class rather than ethnicity, with 28 per cent of the lowest social classes saying there should be less support [for immigrants] whatever the circumstances, compared to 11 per cent of the highest classes'.[1] For it is members of the poorest class — for whom the Tories no longer feel patrician responsibility and Blair's Labour Party no longer feels love — that see their places in queues for housing 'bumped' down to make room at the list's head for newly arrived 'asylum seekers', by people that travelled over many safe countries to come to this one. They see their child's class size get bigger and bigger with the arrival of children whose English is so poor that lesson after lesson becomes a language class; children that should not be in the general educational system, but have nowhere else to go. Their boroughs are ruled by gangs of youths on the streets, youths that see themselves as cultural warriors against the nation that has taken them in, youths that — in the way of gangs everywhere — make this or that place 'theirs' and fight others, fight white youths who are accused of racism for their behaviour but whose revolting behaviour actually arises from a tribalism perfectly mirrored in that of the ethnic minority group concerned, whose banding together is often excused or even applauded as a symbol of minority strength by many in liberal society, particularly in the arts. *Both* are equally revolting. *Both* must be stopped.

---

[1] Bobby Duffy (MORI Social Research Institute) 'Free Rider Phobia' pp. 16–17 in *Prospect* February 2004, p. 17.

This does not affect the middle class. They are screened from much of the damage done by these attitudes by the buffer their comparative wealth gives them. They are protected by postcode, as the areas they live in are not affected by the mass arrival of newcomers nearly so much. On the whole they are not reliant on the instruments of the social safety net. For them, multiculturalism has been an abstract ideal, easily ascribed to because it hardly changes anything in their lives.

But it may come to affect them in very tangible ways. Cultural commonality underpins welfare systems. Erode that commonality too quickly, attempt to change it to benefit newcomers without corresponding tangible benefit to longer-term citizens, and racial tension is an inevitable result. Broadly speaking, I do not object to paying to build a safety net when it protects you and not me, if you are 'like me' and I see that it could just as well benefit me in turn on another occasion. But if that high level of commitment to a welfare system seems designed solely to benefit those who seem so different to me, and have not contributed themselves, I am less likely to wish to contribute to it myself. It is for this reason that the most generous and traditionally liberal of European nations, the Scandinavian countries, now see both great racial tension and a growing opposition to the high level of their social welfare system. For

> herein lies the progressive dilemma of the 21st century. Solidarity and diversity are both desirable concepts. Unfortunately, they can also conflict. A sense of solidarity creates a readiness to share with strangers, which in turn underpins a thriving welfare state. But it is easier to feel solidarity with those who broadly share your values and way of life ... in the 1940s and 1950s, the early days of the welfare state, this was not such an issue. People believed that they were paying the social welfare part of their taxes to people who were like themselves and who faced the same risks and problems. For most people, paying tax was a kind of enlightened self-interest.[2]

This is no longer the case. It is unrealistic and unreasonable to expect taxpayers to have 'the same feelings of generosity or solidarity towards a refugee from the other side of the world as we do towards our next-door neighbour'[3] — until they point comes where we feel they *are* our neighbour, rather than a member of an intrusive element that refuses to assimilate. For 'if the ties that bind you to

---

[2]   Wolfe, Alan and Jytte Klausen 'Other People' pp. 28–33 in *Prospect* December 2000, p. 28.

[3]   Ibid.

increasingly diverse fellow citizens are loosened, you are likely to be less inclined to share your resources with them.'[4]

A community needs 'a common culture, because, without it, it is not a community at all'.[5] But we are losing our common culture. Many individuals consider themselves to be Muslim or Pakistani (for pointed example) before being British. 'If groups within the nation state receive greater recognition, it must follow that conceptions of over-arching national solidarity must receive less.'[6]

The first, obvious point is that we have allowed ourselves to be kowtowed by political correctness from standing up for our own way of life: a civil, liberal, law-abiding *British* way of life that, if strong enough, could happily assimilate immigration even at the very high level at which it currently runs. Beyond this, the middle class specifically is at fault here in two regards — in accepting liberal attitudes about the right to control our borders (i.e. that it doesn't really exist), and in developing a dislike, distrust and disdain for their own national identity: they adopt and promote the throwing off of pride in Britain.

Recently, a prominent member of liberal, clubbish, new-middle class London society said this:

> Statues and monuments are not the sort of thing that get me excited. England is full of statues to people who did revolting things but are feted for their bravery and Christian rectitude. They are everywhere: Churchill, Queen Victoria, Wellington … [In my family] our scorn was reserved for the symbols of Englishness. We would not merely miss the Queen's Speech on Christmas Day. We waited until it got to 3 pm so that we could turn the TV off and deliberately not watch it. Even when we watched *It's a Knockout* we would cheer anyone but the English.[7]

The person that said this was Gary Younge. Mr Younge had just been appointed as the head of the commission set up to decide what should occupy the empty plinth in Trafalgar Square.[8]

In general terms, one questions the wisdom of appointing a man who disdains statues and monuments to a position that involves selecting them. But furthermore, is it not remarkable that such a person is chosen to guide the development of symbolism in this, a quintessentially and uniquely patriotic place at the heart of our nation's capital? As a nation, we are alone in the world in entering

---

[4]   Ibid.
[5]   Tawney, RH *Equality* (London, 1931).
[6]   Wolfe, Alan and Jytte Klausen op cit p. 29.
[7]   Gary Younge as quoted in The Week 18/5/02, extract from *The Daily Mail*.
[8]   A position he has since resigned.

into this communal self-loathing, certainly to the degree to which it is practised here.

Rather than kowtowing to those that say all cultures are equal, or running down our own, we should seek to stress the benefits of the British way of life, whilst striving to amend its faults — otherwise, why do we have it? Indeed, all cultures are *not* equal. It is greatly to the credit of the western world, of which Britain with her strong liberal tradition has traditionally been a strong leader, that women and members of minority communities are so empowered here. It is not so elsewhere. Peter Tatchell's provocative position — that he opposes the spread of the Muslim faith because 'Islam kills queers'[9] — throws the liberal world into paroxysms of logical contortion: assertion of homosexual rights *good*, condemnation of another culture *bad*.

Rather than attempting to square such a logical position with a desire to offer sops to other cultures, we should be willing to assert the primacy of our way of life. We should be proud of our freedom, of our liberality — and we should seek to promulgate them through the promotion of our culture's merits, both abroad and within our own country. We should re-educate our own citizens, in particular our middle class (a former bastion of this certainty, but no longer) about the virtues of the way of life they are fortunate enough to take for granted. For to entertain too much the notion that all cultures are equally valid is to gradually undermine our own, and to open the door — even here, in Britain — to the subjugation of women within the home, to the re-emergence of polygamy and arranged marriages, to honour killings: for there are sub-cultures within Britain's cities and towns that would dearly like to see such practices openly re-established.

Nations are entitled to their own culture and way of life. This is a country that believes in democracy, in the emancipation of all over 18, in the equality of women, in the rule of law. We ought to be proud of this culture, and teach our children to be proud of it too. We shouldn't shirk this important responsibility for fear of offending foreigners — they do the same, and puzzle at our failure to do so.

---

[9]   Peter Tatchell in *The Daily Mail* 'Why I defend this man's right to call gays like me immoral … (even though I don't agree with a single word he says)' p. 26 *The Daily Mail* 26th May 2002.

The Social Contract

Citizenship is not a one-way street. It is a pact, a social contract between state and individual — and obligations lie not merely on the state, but on both parties. In that bargain, the individual should integrate with and support his country, in return for residence, succour in times of trouble and protection from foreign threats. Individuals must not be allowed to form into special interest communities and organisations cut off from the state at large, taking its benefits whilst sneering at and undermining (passively and actively) its way of life.

In the 2004 MORI poll referred to above, that showed that '28 per cent of the lowest social classes saying there should be less support [for immigrants] whatever the circumstances, compared to 11 per cent of the highest classes', 'very few people cited established minorities — Asian people or black people' — as groups to be feared or resented. These groups have been integrated into British society over time — have 'earned' their right to both full citizenship and self-defined distinctness, through hard work and support for the society that accepts them. This is borne out in studies: '86 per cent [of British people] disagree with the idea that you need to be white to be British'.[10] Once, Asians and blacks were not seen as being part of British society; now they are. That is a progression any group accepting British values could mirror — but it must happen over time. The state has a duty to its current citizens to slow down immigration to a pace with which they can cope.

Furthermore, also to safeguard the interests of the current population, there must be some point at which immigration, to any significant degree, must stop. We currently experience net immigration of at least 200,000 people a year.[11] Common sense dictates that there must be some given point of maximum population, beyond which the quality of life for those already here declines to an unacceptable level. The Government accepts no such thing. But surely, simply as a matter of logic, this is true at *some* point? Admittedly, great disagreement would still occur: they might say that level is at some distant point in the future, whilst I would say we cruised through it several years ago; but let's admit that it *exists*.

---

[10] Ibid.
[11] David Goodhart 'Foreword' in *Prospect* February 2003.

Having the Debate

These are compelling issues for the future of our country. But before they can be tackled, we've got to get over the biggest barrier to this discussion — the idea that it simply can't be discussed. For, as on the one hand we become more ethnically and culturally diverse, on the other our opinions are becoming more homogenous in its political correctness and traditional values disappear;[12] our middle class increasingly depends on society at large, channelled though the liberal media, to tell it what to *think*, too — a mawkish, 'PC' righteousness has formed in which no judgment is cast, and none are condemned. At least, this is true in a conventional sense — lawbreakers now longer deserve condemnation but instead can only be helped and understood. Now, the only area in which condemnation really occurs is that of thought — to be labelled 'racist' is the worst damnation society now offers; in this cheap, easy slur 'the ruling class has acquired a term of venomous abuse that can silence most criticism'[13] which has helped pro-immigrationists to successfully avoid the debate on immigration for the last thirty years, during which time they've had things entirely their way. We should be willing to *have* this discussion.

Asylum

A political class terrified of being accused of 'playing the race card' has resulted in collective, consensual silence and inaction on an issue of great importance — Britain's asylum and refugee policy.

The granting of asylum, or the failure to deport those refused it, is running at such a high level that asylum impacts on the macro picture of immigration into Britain generally. However, current policy is more than a semi-masked method of facilitating mass immigration without the consent of the public — it is also profoundly unfair. The UK budget for asylum seekers and refugees is £1.7 billion and we dealt with 103,000 people in 2002.[14] The budget for the whole of the UNHCR programme, which deals with 19.8 million people

---

[12] This is not to suggest that the two strands, more immigration and a shift to homogeneous non-condemnatory thinking, are linked — indeed, immigrants to this country are often aghast at the unwillingness to enforce moral judgment on societally damaging behaviour. I observe that these two separate trends have occurred at the same time, and allow pro-immigration thinkers promulgating the first trend to mask their arguments with the intellectual cowardice of the ultimate insult ('you racist') offered by the second.

[13] Sean Gabb *Cultural Revolution, Culture War* London, 2003 p. 26.

[14] Both facts taken from Home Office *News Release* 058/2003.

every year,[15] is USD \$955 million[16] — much less. Those we take in are, for the most part, fit young men[17] with the financial and physical resources to undergo a long and perilous journey, coming via nations in which they could and should claim asylum but choose not to, promulgating a vast criminality on the way — they are those that need our help least. Those that the UNHCR treat are those that abide by the international system and wait where we ask them to, in the camps — they are the sick, the very old, and the very young — they are those that truly need our help. They have done what the international community has asked them to do: they have stayed in the refugee camps and waited for help. Mine is not an argument for a smaller British aid budget — it is a suggestion that the current one is horribly misspent. With blinkers on and a false sense of doing good, we treat those able enough to come to our door. In doing so, we encourage others to follow them and jump the queue too. It will keep happening until we act — act by refusing those with false claims, by automatically turning around those that come to us via safe nations in which they would have stopped. To do so will not only be to secure our own borders. Given that we necessarily have a finite pot from which to dispense monies for asylum seekers and refugees, which will thereafter not be spent in this inequitable way, it will also be to help those that need us most.

Patriotism

The middle class once, with some very few liberal exceptions, marched in step with the working class on this issue; widespread patriotism marked all aspects British life. I would contend that this is a signature of national wellbeing. But it has now abandoned its position as sceptical guardian of the British social dynamic — only 49% of Britons say they are very proud of their nationality, compared with 72% of Americans.[18]

As a part of the Golden Jubilee celebrations of 2002, The Queen visited East London on 9th May and met the ceremonial mayor of Newham, Councillor Sukdev Singh Marway. Many striking photographs emerged from this day — of this great tall turbaned man

[15] 'Refugee Women' *UNHCR in the UK* 2003:
    http://www.unhcr.org.uk/info/briefings/asylum_issues/women.html
[16] 'Refugee funding worries Southern Agencies' ReliefWeb.com 24th September 2003: *http://www.reliefweb.int/w/rwb.nsf/0/42fd08fa7ab1e16749256 dac000035c6?OpenDocument*
[17] Richard Smith 'Q&A Asylum: Myths or Truths?' *BBC News Online* 22nd July 2003: *http://news.bbc.co.uk/1/hi/england/3087615.stm*
[18] Anatol Lieven 'Demon in the Cellar' pp 28-33 in *Prospect* March 2004 p. 30.

standing with a living symbol of British tradition and social conti-
nuity, both smiling warmly at the pleasure of the other's company,
whilst all around them many British Sikhs and Muslims applauded,
waving their Union Jacks. On that day, as so often in the celebrations of Her Majesty's Jubilee, support for more than the monarchy
was affirmed — support for the values of British morality and aspiration was evoked, too — often from quarters for which British
intellectual opinion presumes to speak, when preaching of the
needs of 'minorities' in a culture supposedly set against them.

Indeed, it is often newcomers to Britain who most *want* to live in
communities with a sense of social discipline, attracted as they were
by Britain's largely false image held abroad as a country characterised by social wellbeing, benevolent support for the instruments of
law and order, of traditional standards of medical care and sound
schooling practice; many immigrants are disappointed by the abandonment of long-held values and trendy unwillingness to condemn
others that characterise today's middle class, and by the real social
harm that follows it. Industrious immigrants, willing to work hard
for just reward, drawn to Britain by their aspiration to live in a successful country that supposedly enshrines values of respect and
care for our fellow man that are admired the world over, often sur-
prise social commentators with their disappointment with modern
'multicultural' Britain. For, in seeking a 'multicultural society', we
have abandoned the great strengths of British culture that have
attracted those from other cultures to come to this country in the
first place.

The response to problems with achieving harmony between races
in these islands should not be to destroy Britishness, but to convince
minorities that they *are* British, to accept Britishness. Traditions and
customs offer the *best* hope of harmony existing, not a stumbling
block to it. Without unifying the races in Britishness, what remains
are blood ties, kith and kin, which will see our country truly rent
into factions that live apart and fear each other: when there is no
shared national identity, upheld by common customs, then race
becomes more important, not less. The distinction was made neatly
by the late Pim Fortuyn, who was in favour of multiracialism, but
against multiculturalism.

Thus, the introduction of citizenship classes and ceremonies for
those becoming citizens is wonderful. There is, though, irony in the
fact that under this government immigrants to the United Kingdom
are now taught in citizenship classes the very values the middle

class has systematically abandoned, values they were urged to abandon by this same government.

This effort to instil a common sense of Britishness has significant opponents. In the aftermath of events such as the murder of Stephen Lawrence, there has been clamour for the dismantling of the institutions of traditional Britain (often from groups that have an interest in society being split, as its leaders make their living from discussing and stirring it). When Benjamin Zephaniah refused to accept an honour from the Crown, he undermined the notion of inclusive Britishness, and sent a message of peculiarly unpleasant rejection to the country that has accepted him and wished to honour him, and to the many millions born here upon whom no such honours are bestowed. Meanwhile, the recent recommendation from MPs to change the honours system,[19] to destroy something around which we could all rally as Britons, is spuriously based on the idea that such honours are someone not 'inclusive' of some groups... something that is in some perverse way true for as long as people refuse them, I suppose.

Nevertheless, though many will continue to mock and jeer the idea of Britishness, we should persevere with the attempt to engender it in all our citizens. Few things depend as much as this on the middle class. Few tasks facing society are more important.

---

[19] 'Honours system outdated, says MP' *BBC Online* 13th July 2004: *http://news.bbc.co.uk/1/hi/uk_politics/3888581.stm*

Chapter 6

The Fruit of the Abdication: Crime

Today's political agenda is no longer about finding a compromise between socialism and capitalism. Increasingly the new politics is about moderating behaviour and re-establishing the social virtues of self-discipline coupled with an awareness of the needs of others. It is these virtues above all others that are essential to civilized living. The new politics centre on reinforcing what is good and acceptable behaviour.

Frank Field[1]

Serious crime has steadily risen in this country for two generations.

This is so according to evidence provided by the Home Office on 'long-term trends in national recorded crime'.[2] There has been no downturn over the last ten years, as is sometimes claimed. The only crimes on the decline are those that improving technology makes more difficult to commit — burglaries and car thefts are combated by better locks, security alarms (and, in some areas, private security). Furthermore, the decline in value of 'burglable' goods such as DVD players makes burgling less profitable, so a certain amount of displacement occurs in the statistics as burglars move on to other crimes such as muggings.[3] There is therefore no real credit to be gained by politicians or law enforcers from the decline in burglary: it merely represents victims getting better at defending themselves, and some crimes becoming less attractive, in an environment that is innately more criminal and more violent.

---

[1]   Frank Field *Neighbours from Hell: the Politics of Behaviour* (London, 2003).
[2]   John Steele 'Trends reveal rising tide of violence' *The Daily Telegraph* 20th July 2004 p. 4. The statistics that follow come from this article.
[3]   'The decline of the English burglary' p. 31 *The Economist* 29th May 2004.

This is borne out by the government's own statistics on other crimes. Gun crime has more than doubled since 1997.[4] Muggings, serious violence, rape, possession of drugs: all are much more common now than they were before the turn of the century. This is lamentable. But of even more concern is crime that is *not* serious, crimes that go unreported, crimes that occur by the tens of thousand every day. Much of it is mindless destruction and vandalism. With minor crimes such as these, there is (even) less chance of catching the perpetrators. Petty crime, and the environment of antagonism and aggression that spawns it, contribute enormously to the way individuals feel about their community.

At its most grave extreme, the environment of commonplace petty crime is reflected in the number of violent disorder offences ('a disturbance made by an unruly mob of three people or more'), which doubled in the period from 1993 to 2003. Similarly, figures for damage to vehicles show a similarly large escalation. However, most 'environment-crimes' go unreported — unreported as far as the authority is concerned, but not within the community, where the tales of individual victims permeate the atmosphere and contribute to the malaise British society is experiencing.

Every month in Britain, a country with one of the worst crime rates in Europe,[5] sees terrible events occur — they happen so regularly that unless we really concentrate, our eyes slip over them on the newspaper, not really taking them in. For instance, a small example of how vicious crime is so commonplace in modern Britain that it has become mundane is to be found on page six of the *Daily Telegraph* on the 20th July 2004. Story one is 'Elderly couple killed trying to protect their own home'; story two is 'Man sought over murder of twins'.[6]

A single murder was once front page news in this country. Here are two double murders tucked in at page six, the combined space devoted to them less than that given to the 'story' about summer punting in Cambridge on the facing page.

---

[4]   Interestingly, this has occurred *after* the 1996 ban on handguns following Dunblaine, and after 160,000 handguns were handed in to police stations during the amnesty that followed.

[5]   'Labour crime crackdown has failed, says report' p. 7 *Sunday Times* 13th February 2005.

[6]   Between the time at which the paper was printed and when it appeared on the newsstands, it emerged that the same suspect was believed to have committed both double murders: *BBC Online* 'Man Hunted for Four Murders' 20th July 2004:
http://news.bbc.co.uk/1/hi/england/north_yorkshire/3909539.stm

Also in that month, in New Cross, a boy of 14 killed his 15-year-old brother over scratches on a compact disc.[7] In a dispute between neighbours in Littlehampton, one mother stabbed her neighbour, another mother, to death because of music the victim's daughter was playing in her room.[8]

When huge, revolting crimes are common, the petty crime we have all experienced goes all-but unnoticed (and most often, unreported). Anti-social behaviour plagues communities, despite the Anti-Social Behaviour Orders (ASBOs) about 1,500 of which are now made every year. Many have seen their community decline from law abiding to crime-ridden in their own lifetime.

The sad story of the life and death of Paul Wardell spoke to many in that situation. Mr Wardell stood up for himself, and for those around him. He challenged the yobs and thugs on his Teesside estate when they preyed on the vulnerable. In revenge, he was viciously beaten by four of them, in front of his young son. They used baseball bats and weapons bought from martial arts shops. His skull was fractured. When the case against his attackers collapsed, he took his own life.[9]

Whilst it went unnoticed amongst the powers that be, this vignette of modern life was much discussed amongst people in places like those in which Mr Wardell lived. Even worse than the widespread recognition of the environment outlined in Mr Wardell's story was the resignation many felt — that this is simply the way life is now conducted in large parts of modern Britain.

This is the fruit borne of the modern-day liberalism prevalent in the politics of crime. This kind of situation, seen all over Britain, that has come from the unwillingness to confront the worst issues of British life, because they involve unpalatable truths about the wrong-headedness of so much of twentieth-century social policy. This, lived out on the estates of Britain's poor, is the logical result of the self-indulgence of Britain's middle class in abandoning its support for traditional law and order. And this is what Mr Blair meant when — far, far too late — he made his much-maligned speech on the follies of 1960s thinking.

The spread of crime damages society as a whole, and makes its restoration so much harder. The force of this dilemma should not be underestimated, for it has done for societies older than our own: 'as

---

[7]   Sue Clough 'Boy who killed brother over CD can go home' *The Daily Telegraph* 31st July 2004.

[8]   David Sapsted 'Neighbour stabbed to death over daughter's loud music' *The Daily Telegraph* 24th July 2004.

[9]   Jenny Johnston 'Street of fear' pp. 28–29 *The Daily Mail* 4th September 2004.

the violence spread it brought a collapse in the habits, institutions, beliefs, and restraints that are the foundations of civilized life.'[10]

The Prime Minister recently admitted that anti-social behaviour is making life 'hell' for many.[11] It is excellent that the state is now acknowledging the dilemma. However, it is wrong that the easy route of undermining the norms of justice has been taken, rather than tackling the root cause of the problem, which is the total lack of respect for authority in the groups that produce the individual offenders concerned. For ASBOs are civil law orders, requiring a lower standard of proof than criminal offences, able to rely on hearsay evidence, and to be imposed before an individual actually commits an offence. Many civil libertarians object. Whilst acknowledging the force of their objections I am nevertheless in favour of the orders, as the situation is so bad that in the short term action must be taken despite such qualms. But no matter how harsh the orders are, of themselves they cannot fashion change in the way that we behave, and they cannot hope to stem the tide of unpleasantness which surely manifests itself in hundreds of thousands of incidents a year, rather than one thousand. A respect for authority, discipline in our schools (and support for those that enforce it) — these must be the aims. Without that, the behaviour ASBOs are intended to combat will continue, and continue to make living in our communities, in the Prime Minister's words, 'hell'.

Consider the case of William Sutcliffe, beaten by three men in the toddler's enclosure at Hampstead Heath whilst he and his friend supervised his year-old son at play:

> A five-year-old boy carrying a large pump-action machine gun-style water pistol appeared, squirted my friend in the crotch, and said: 'Ha ha, you've pissed yourself …' We heard him say to his friend: 'Let's get the baby.' I stood up sharply and positioned myself between my son and the boy with the gun, who continued to rush at me, even though I was blocking his path. His body briefly came into contact with my outstretched arms and he fell rather melodramatically flat onto his back … as I was bending to help the child, who was not even slightly hurt or upset, I saw a large man in his late twenties running towards me with his fist clenched, followed by two of his friends. The next thing I knew, I had been punched in the head and shoved to the ground. This gang of men was now kicking me in the head and chest … I found myself saying simply, 'I'm sorry, I'm sorry.'

---

[10] Donald Kagan *The Peloponnesian War* London, 2003 p. xxv.
[11] Toby Helm 'Blair and Howard put battle against yobs at forefront of election' p. 9 *The Daily Telegraph* 1st September 2004.

No one should have to endure this kind of behaviour. But in truth, this account was notable only in that it happened to a journalist, capable in some way of calling attention to his utterly mundane experience. Sutcliffe's reaction to his experience is one in accord with the retreat of the middle class all over Britain:

> Until last Saturday, I had intended to send my son to the local school, which I now realise he might share with machine gun boy and his charming father. I had wanted him to be part of the community in which we live. Now, like other cowardly members of the middle classes, I am re-examining my bank balance. If hard cash — and a private education — is what it takes for him to believe that he lives in a society where the word prevails over the fist, it will be money well spent.

This is entirely understandable. But the boy *won't* live in a society where the word prevails over the fist — merely in a peaceable bubble within a society where the fist's reign is unquestioned.

The retreat of the law-abiding behind their doors and off the streets in the evening (and even daytime) represents the victory of the criminal against society at large. When the monied class begins shutting itself away in 'gated communities' one is alarmed, but those with a great deal of property to lose have always feared crime more. Now, citizens in every class of society fear crime, and even those with little money to spare turn to security measures once unthought-of. The people of the small, and by no means wealthy, village of Ryton-on-Dunsmore, for example — ironically, located near Warwickshire's large police training centre — has hired a private security company to police its streets, so constant is the petty crime that plagues them.[12]

We — the middle class — have no real right to lament this state of affairs, as we are responsible for it. The terrible division of decent society into those that can afford to buy peace and those that cannot is our fault. We turn away when we should speak. When children misbehave, we don't discipline them. When we see youths throwing stones, spraying graffiti, breaking something, we do nothing. Children who go unpunished for bullying, rudeness and damaging the property of others grow up to be violent, abusive vandals. Vandals who go unrebuked move on to yet worse deeds. It is the middle class's unwillingness to fight the destruction of discipline in schools that has allowed the classroom to become a place of fear. Because the enemy of proper teaching comes with words of equality and provision for all, because our way of life is being killed with appar-

[12] Nick Britten 'Villagers "let down" by local force will hire private eyes to do the job' *The Daily Telegraph* 22nd July 2004.

ent kindness, we haven't fought it. In fact, many of our number led the charge. In the current climate it would be very hard for individuals to act even if willing to, because the sense that the community will support him in his intervention is lacking: when the yobs on the underground turn on the man who speaks out, others hide behind their papers and avoid eye contact. So we can hardly complain when forced to buy the security we once would have had at no expense — forced to protect ourselves by buying homes in safer areas, to protect our children by paying for private schooling. Instead, our sympathy should be with those poor souls that can't take that option — and are condemned to live in the world without rules that we have created.

Punishment

The government's response to rising crime has been to create new offences in law — 270 since 1997, in fact.[13] But if the will to properly enforce laws does not exist, this achieves nothing: the new laws go as unnoticed as the old ones, which would have served perfectly well if actually applied. Traditionally, the middle class has recognised with admirable common sense that harsh penalties are required to act as a deterrent to crime. Yet at the urging of the metropolitan liberal elite, a thoroughly middle class grouping, we are abandoning the idea that criminals are accountable for their actions: rather, we have come to 'treat crime as the symptom of a social and economic disease, requiring treatment rather than penalties'.[14] This is inherently to the disadvantage of the middle class, whose liberal sensibilities seem to be propelling it, as

> the more bureaucratic and formal the criminal justice system becomes, the less use it will be against the disorderly and disobedient. Such people treat a prison record as a career risk, do not pay fines (huge amounts are uncollected, although the middle class still tend to pay), fail to turn up to court or do not stay long at the same address. It is then simpler and more convenient for the police to pursue the settled and orderly members of society. They are easy to find, can have their regular earnings raided to pay fines and still fear the stigma of a criminal record.[15]

More gravely, the removal of responsibility from criminals, and the subsequent masochistic bearing of the burden by society as a whole, damages the liberties and freedoms of all the citizens within it. For

[13] 'Blair's criminal intent' p. 19 *The Daily Telegraph* 20th July 2004.
[14] Peter Hitchens *The Abolition of Liberty: The Decline of Order and Justice in England* London, 2004 (revised edition) p. 8.
[15] Ibid.

'a society where crime is an endemic disease to be contained and placated needs to treat all of its citizens as potential suspects all the time.'[16] This effectively removes the presumption of innocence, leaving the state fearing all citizens all the time. It is also remarkably inefficient, as 'this approach will only reduce crime when the state becomes all powerful'.[17]

Lashing Out, Without Knowing Why

Displaying a singular lack of self-preservational thought, British society attacks those that, in the most literal of senses, save us from danger. As one firefighter wrote recently, 'I have been the target for yobs throwing stones and punches at me while I do my job.'[18] Emergency vehicles are often called out by gangs of youths who seek to trap them in cul de sacs and pelt them with rocks.

It is true that such widespread gang violence occurs more in poorer areas — so that those that need help most are least likely to get it, as areas become 'no-go' (and thus attract even more trouble). By way of illustration, burglary figures show that, just as middle class desire to 'equalise' in education harms the children in inner city schools the most, the abrogation of proper policing it essentially advocates similarly harms the working class most. Though it affects us all, 'crime hits the poorest hardest. Around five per cent of those earning under £5,000 a year were burgled in 2003–4, compared with approximately 2.7 per cent of those earning more than £30,000.'[19]

However, in this as in much else the middle class apes the behaviour and values of those it has traditionally guided. Yobbery is rife on our streets, its participants middle class as often as working class. Clued-up football thugs now pre-arrange their fights over the internet, applauding the violent efforts of their 'side' and of their opponents in chat rooms.[20] Many live in leafy streets and work as accountants and solicitors by day. The middle class often *participates* in this pursuit — in a real-life *Fight Club* that sees grown men with responsible jobs, with wives and children, co-ordinate gang warfare.

---

[16] Ibid.
[17] Ibid.
[18] Jay Curson, letter to *The Guardian* 19th October 2002.
[19] Institute for Public Policy Research 'A decade of tackling poverty, but Britain's far from a fair society' 2nd August 2004:
        http://www.ippr.org.uk/press/index.php?release=332
[20] Patrick McGowan 'Massive swoop on the website soccer thugs' *Evening Standard* 24th October 2002.

Such behaviour is not restricted to our shores; indeed, it often forms the predominant impression others abroad have of the British: 'Czech officials privately guess that a quarter of fights in the [Prague] city centre involve British men. There is no way of proving that: British men generally beat up each other, and charges are seldom brought.'[21] As European expansion has opened up new flight routes, Prague has thankfully seen a drop in the huge groups of British men descending on it at weekends, as tour groups such as tallinpissup.com export them to the tiny Baltic States instead.[22] Britain's reputation is not well served by these ambassadors. The groups were welcomed at first, for the money they brought; but they frighten away other tourists and locals alike, leaving tradesmen with an unreliable short term trade from violent young British men, and the generation-long links with their traditional, more sedate tourists from Scandinavia and Germany destroyed.

Is such behaviour due to a lack of fear of its consequences, or a lack of moral awareness?

The Police

The restrictions we have placed on the police force emasculate them. No constable has confidence that he will be supported in a lawsuit laid against him — naturally enough, since Britain's has become a culture based on rights, rather than on responsibilities. This cripples the force. The policeman should be reassuring to the citizen that keeps the law, and *frightening* to those that contemplate breaking it.

There are more policemen than ever. But those policemen have to do more paperwork than ever. Alarmingly, 'in many places the ratio of backroom staff to patrol officers is roughly 5:1.'[23] The result is that the conviction (or 'clear-up') rate is down to 23%, despite the extra manpower.[24]

This is lamentable. But conviction rates aren't nearly as important as *detection* rates. Criminals are only put off committing crimes by high sentences if they believe they'll be caught in the first place. Even when convictions are not obtained, the mere process of investigation, of knowing that one's criminal activities have come to the

[21] 'Ferrets Abroad' *The Economist* 12th December 2002.
[22] Julius Strauss 'Estonians waking up to life with lager louts' p. 13 *The Daily Telegraph* 7th August 2004.
[23] Gary Mason 'Why you can never find a policeman when you need one' p. 17 *The Daily Express* 26th February 2002.
[24] Philip Johnston 'Extra police but detection rate still falls' p. 8 *The Daily Telegraph* 22nd July 2004.

attention of the authorities, has a salutary effect in and of itself. The only way to improve detection rates is to free up officers to pursue more cases. Requiring multi-page reports on every incident militates against such an aim.

The paperwork folly is both symptom and partial cause of the 'fire station policing' now common in policing today. Police emerge sirens blazing from the station when a crime has already been committed, rather than walk the streets. For the law-abiding, this style of policing creates precisely the reverse of the intended result:

> The wailing, tyre-screeching presence ... provides no reassurance. In fact, it does just the opposite, acting as a daily reminder of violent crime.[25]

The police are very different from the fire brigade. Their mere presence acts as a deterrent to the thing they exist to combat. The fire brigade exists to tackle something that is always (or at least, *should* always be) created by accident or neglect: so the 'station house' plan makes sense. The police exist not only to tackle crime when it occurs, but also to be present in the hearts and minds of the community as a source of reassurance for some and a disincentive to commit crime for others. To do both, it has to be a visible force, and be visible *before* the crime occurs.

That visibility relies on policemen being known to the community they police, rather than periodically imposing themselves on it in times of trouble and then retreating once more behind the fortress door. This has become even more unlikely as we have removed not only the constables but also the stations themselves from many communities. In the last ten years, 800 police stations have closed and only 250 have opened.[26]

This is precisely opposite to the desired trend in policing – the force should be *closer* to the community, not further away. That closeness is the first of two elements needed to tackle crime by making it less likely before the fact, rather than pursuing it afterwards.

> The guiding vision for law enforcement must be to maintain order within each city, not to catch criminals. Creating an environment that is not conducive to illegality, rather than seeking to punish illegal conduct after the fact, is the key to preventing crime.[27]

---

[25] Mason op cit.
[26] Philip Johnston 'Case of the missing police stations' p. 2 *The Daily Telegraph* 10th August 2004,
[27] George L Kelling and Ronald Corbett 'This Works: Preventing and Reducing Crime' *Civic Bulletin*, No 32 March 2003: Center for Civic Innovation at the Manhattan Institute p. 1.

To do that, we must cultivate in a society that has respects the law and those that enforce it, in order to engender an environment that is innately law-abiding rather than lawless.

The second limb is the responsibility we bear *ourselves* to protect the community from wrongdoers. It is here, even more than in the woeful state of modern police practice, that we fail.

It is not only the case that we require more police because there is more crime, though that is obviously true. We also require more police because we have shorn the law-abiding community of any ability to take action itself. We are afraid to attempt to stop children behaving criminally because they are violent. But we are also afraid of children because if we do attempt to stop them behaving criminally, we are likely to be arrested ourselves.

'Direct action' or 'having a go' need not be the only way one can act for the betterment of the community. Reporting crimes, 'keeping an eye out' — being aware of and caring about what's happening in our neighbourhood — these things are vital too. It is certainly true that commentators still *think* that the middle class does this. 'If one had to make a sweeping generalisation about the middle classes, it would be that we are a respectable, non-violent, politically disparate, occasionally blinkered race of do-gooders.'[28] If only it were so. To be fair, one recognises the people of Lewis' portrait, who do indeed still exist — they are the middle-aged teachers, plumbers, doctors and nurses, the mechanics and builders, of Britain's market towns and suburbia. But these are also the people that lock themselves away in fear at night. These are the people who refuse to condemn others, and whose 'do-gooding' instinct is swiftly being blunted. And, applying another sweeping generalisation, none of the qualities apply to an important subset of the middle classes — their children.

The Dissolute Society

When one voices concerns about the dissolute state of society, one is often told, 'it was like this in Dickens!' To these generalisations, I reply, the works of Dickens document a searing poverty. Why does such behaviour occur *now*, when that excuse is no longer available? Furthermore, positing, with suitable pseudo-learned expression, that there were street gangs in London in the 1800s and so forth may seem clever and is allows commentator to give easy answers on

---

[28]   Jemima Lewis 'Bourgeois and proud of it' *The Daily Telegraph* 25th August 2004.

radio shows — but such an approach seems glib and ignorant to those who *know*, because they have witnessed it in their own lifetimes, that there has been 'an palpable decline in the standards of public behaviour' — an inevitable result of 'the shift from a largely authoritarian culture to a permissive culture in the space of half a lifetime'.[29]

Poverty breeds habits and these habits breed the bitterness that inevitably comes with them: the social implications go on and on, often beyond the point at which the cause no longer exists. This is true of blacks in America's inner cities, whose culture has yet to recover from the experience of slavery: the problem facing the white working class is that there's no distinctive feature that compels class sympathy and understanding, no cataclysmic, attention-holding event to explain or justify its state. It may simply be that great elements of the working class have yet to shrug off the habits of bitterness, rejection of societal rules and the criminality that stems from these two things, habits engendered by the poverty endured by their forefathers but in the main no longer felt by themselves.

The real question is: why does the *middle* class behave like this? Standards have been inverted. Public drunkenness is a sign of belonging, of being 'all right'. Especially amongst the young, binge drinking is encouraged.

The increasing trend of excessive consumption applies (uniquely to Britain, it seems) as much to girls as to boys — indeed, research conducted by Exeter University in 2004 produced results that suggest that amongst 14 and 15 year olds, girls now drink and smoke even more than boys (with almost half of all children of both sexes in that age group drinking regularly).[30] The Office of National Statistics reports that the number of young women drinking above safe limits has more than doubled from one in 10 in 1988-89 to one in six in 2002-03.[31] British women hold the dubious title of biggest drinkers in Europe (with a level of average consumption fully double that of nations such as Italy, Sweden or Spain).[32]

This is combined with the appearance of British women at the head of the WHO's worldwide tables of both drug taking and junk

---

[29]   Phil Craig 'Reign of Terror' pp. 12–14 *The Spectator* 4th May 2002.
[30]   Judith O'Reilly 'Schoolgirls beat the boys at drinking' p. 11 *The Sunday Times* 16th August 2004.
[31]   Sarah Womack 'The 'lager ladette' culture doubles in 10 years' *The Daily Telegraph* 30th July 2004.
[32]   India Knight 'Girls behaving madly' p. 4 News Review *The Sunday Times* 26th September 2004.

food consumption[33] to make the state of health amongst our young women truly woeful. Even discounting the long-term effects on health of this, the results are seen in our casualty departments every week: injuries from women involved in fights following binge-drinking, including the terrible injuries associated with 'glassing', have risen sharply, and continue to do so — in many areas of Britain the number of admissions has tripled over five years.[34]

But — obviously — the dramatic change in the habits of young women in this country has an effect beyond the purely physical: it has a huge deleterious effect on the nature of our society. A blind eye has been turned to the appalling activity of many British women because it is somehow seen as the price of liberation. Perhaps this is why, whilst criticism of this cycle of binge drinking is now in vogue, much of it continues to be made on health grounds. But this is more than a health problem. These girls and women are behaving shamefully.

Even discounting the serious risk of violence in venturing out at night, when visitors from abroad see the 'mooning' and vomiting so popular of an evening in many of our towns, one feels ashamed to belong to the same nation as these totally classless women, who swagger out into the night in microskirts, caked with make-up, with the aim of getting 'plastered'. Anonymous and near-anonymous intercourse naturally abounds in such an environment. Britain's permanent place at the head of the teen pregnancy tables also owes something to it, as does the crisis in sexual health outlined in Chapter Three.

We could once look to the behaviour of women to exert a civilizing influence on culture. As long as the attitude prevails that this kind of 'ladette' activity is 'cool' and not to be admonished, that will not be the case in Britain, which is particularly regrettable since we are a country that desperately needs just such a civilising influence.

In this field, government is all-but powerless. Loutishness, incivility, a culture of binge drinking, a widespread debasement of the body through the popular conception of intercourse without repercussion or real meaning: none of these things — which reinforce one another — are suited to government intervention. Whilst it is certainly true that those in power should set a good example rather

---

[33]   India Knight op cit.
[34]   Julie Henry and Michael Day '"Ladettes" clog casualty units after catfights' p. 15 *The Sunday Telegraph* 19th September 2004.

than a bad one,[35] active promotion of civil behaviour may actually undermine that goal: condemnation by authority figures will only make the thing one wishes to stop become more attractive. It is up to individuals — particularly, to strong-minded, young individuals — to ensure that the appropriate stigma is once again applied to the self-demeaning bingeing that is so fashionable.

The repulsive culture that has of late taken hold of many British girls is in part a reflection of the more widespread belief, unique to this country, that one drinks to get drunk — that the measure of an evening is how ill one has made oneself.

The long-term repercussions are obvious. Unless we begin to seriously hold individual drinkers responsible for their actions, and punish those that transgress social norms because of alcohol, society will either buckle completely or become more intolerant of that cause per se — and access to alcohol will be limited by, for example, higher prices and a raise in the drinking age. All, including responsible drinkers, will suffer collectively for the failure to combat irresponsible individuals.

This is true of the problems facing society more widely. Paradoxically, freedom depends upon restraint: unless self-discipline is present in the exercise of freedom, one can destroy it. But many people seem not to believe this. The central concern here might be said to be the difference between liberalism and libertarianism. As Jonathan Sachs puts it: 'for liberalism, freedom is collective self-government and morality consists at least in part in those virtues that support it. For libertarianism, by contrast, freedom is the protection of individual choice.' Thus, 'liberals took for granted that freedom depended upon self-discipline. Libertarians decided that all such restraint was repressive.'[36] But in the final analysis society has to be able to *function*. If we continue to push at the margins of permissibility, unrestrained by any sense of moral norms, we threaten the survival of the very freedoms people revel in.

This is the macro concern: on a micro level, the individual demeans himself by failing to exercise moral restraint. This is so in

---

[35] How can we expect the populace at large to be civil, when those that ought to set an example are not? To give a well-known example of boorishness, the Deputy Prime Minister, John Prescott, put two fingers up to the press at the moment of entering 10 Downing Street. The most remarkable thing about the event was that no-one was surprised. (*BBC Online* 'John Prescott's Gift of the Gaffe' 6th June 2003):
http://news.bbc.co.uk/1/hi/uk_politics/2968074.stm

[36] Melanie Phillips op cit. The Jonathan Sachs quotation is also drawn from this essay.

the sexual arena, in which individuals should hold their bodies in high regard, hold themselves in high regard, and believe that they are worth more than the casual denigration of themselves necessarily involved in 'casual' encounters. It is also true that this applies to intoxication, something that most people from time to time enjoy, but that requires the ability to control oneself and restrict such activities to levels of intake and locations to imbibe, which do not lead to publicly humiliating oneself.

Anti-Social Behaviour

A fascinating sign of the state of modern Britain is the introduction and distribution to all bus drivers of so-called DNA 'spit kits'. One approves of the efforts to take a zero tolerance approach to 'social' crimes, and indeed the (formerly extraordinarily high) rate of passengers and members of the public spitting on drivers and staff have plummeted since the arrival, and first successful prosecution resulting from, the 'spit recovery kits'.[37] But what are we to think of a society in which people spit at one another so often that they're necessary?

Britain is a depressing country to live in. An atmosphere of depression, despondency and pessimism reigns, one more suitable for a poor nation with high unemployment than for a large, successful one with low unemployment. This is largely because of anti-social behaviour. The culture of saying hello, of thanking others for service, holding open a door or allowing one to pass, has all-but disappeared. We push, shove, snarl. To live in a British city is to experience constant incivility. In fact, this extends more and more to country towns, too.

'Nothing really matters more to the quality of our lives than the way we treat one another, than our capacity to live respectfully together as a unified society, with a full, generous regard for the rights of others and also for the feelings of others.'[38] The lack of such regard is always on display in Britain — for example, on the streets. Frequently, groups of people take up the whole of the pavement, forcing others to step into the road to get around them. Sometimes, especially in late evenings, these groups consist of aggressive drunks. But most often they consist of people who are merely inconsiderate, uncaring — so absorbed in themselves that they ignore or are blind to the needs of those around them. Often drivers, includ-

---

[37] Paul Donald 'DNA Testing Kit leads to conviction and £300 fine' *The Scotsman* 27th October 2004.
[38] Richard Nixon *State of the Union Address* 20th January 1972.

ing bus drivers, simply ignore road signals such as pedestrian cross-ings. Why are our cyclists uniquely incompetent? Even apparently mature adults now seem unable to use a bicycle unless it's on the pavement. This seems accepted to the point that journalists write columns sneering at the harassed pedestrians who protest:

> A Virginia Woolf lookalike — dressed by Greenham Common, art-fully messed-up bird's nest hair streaked with grey — pleaded with me not to ride my bike on the pavement. 'You can't, you just can't,' she screeched, dragging at my cuff. Pointing to my earphones, I mimed a 'Sorry, I can't hear you', and sailed on down the pave-ment.[39]

From the mildest of examples such as this one, we see that incivility is the norm in British life. These things build up, day by day. We are sworn at by the driver. Jeered at by the schoolchildren. Are forced to avert our eyes on the tube or on the street as the thug leers. So people feel unsafe or unhappy, though nothing has 'happened' to them.

We are told that the facts — crime statistics and so forth — run against this, and that we should look at the facts, not how people feel. But feelings are very important. Feelings, fears, attitudes about others: these things are governed as much by the *impression* of the world around us as its actual nature. Apparently, the chance of being seriously assaulted is still very low. The level of fear of such an attack is huge. This is so despite the number of policemen in the UK being at the highest level ever.

You don't have to be attacked to be a victim. We are all victims of the unpleasantness of the British urban environment, of 'the great British high street: grubby, smoggy, chip paper-strewn, full of kids on skateboards, mums with sharp-edged shoppers and spitting teenagers'.[40] We ought to be able to live in an environment that isn't soured by anti-social behaviour and crime. People ought to be able to walk down the street late at night without being accosted by drunken, aggressive youths.

We, each of us, have a part to play in solving this. One shouldn't turn a blind eye when someone smashes a telephone box, or sprays graffiti on the wall — and those that do such things should consis-tently be punished. But they are not, and such acts occur every day, and go unpunished. We habitually ignore acts and forms of behav-iour that aren't *crimes*, but make living here very unpleasant – spit-ting gum on the floor, snarling at others on the bus or train. For these

---

[39] Harry Mount 'Diana deserves better than a dried-up lump of granite' *The Daily Telegraph* 22nd July 2004.

[40] Tina Gaudoin 'Coolhunter: Warehouse' p. 15 *The Times Magazine* 5th June 2004.

things profoundly affect our societal morale, and determine to a large extent how the individual feels about the society he lives in.

There is no doubt that there is *some* awareness of these problems, and of the concerns of many people about them: for the first time, the government has 'set out to measure the extent of anti-social behaviour in Britain' in its efforts to enforce Anti-Social Behaviour Orders (ASBOs):

> Nobody quite knows the scale of the problem, hence the Home Office survey, but almost everybody thinks it is growing rapidly. And while it is the poor whose lives are most blighted, few are left untouched. Part of the difficulty of gauging the extent of anti-social behaviour is that much of it does not show up in the usual crime statistics. That may be one reason why people think crime is getting worse when the official figures point in the opposite direction.[41]

As Frank Field puts it:

> [T]he distinguishing mark of anti-social behaviour is that each single instance does not by itself warrant a counter legal challenge. It is in its regularity that anti-social behaviour wields its destructive force. It is from the repetitive nature of the nuisance that anti-social behaviour is born ... it is because such behaviour was, until quite recently, unimaginable that no effective legal remedy exists to counter it.[42]

However, whilst the advent of ASBOs is to be lauded, on the whole it is not the job of government to deal with these issues: it is up to individuals to improve our society.

---

[41] 'The Politics of Behaviour' p. 34 in *The Economist* 13th September 2003.
[42] Frank Field: *Neighbours from Hell: The Politics of Behaviour* as quoted in 'The Politics of Behaviour' in *The Economist* 13th September 2003.

Remotivating the Middle Class

In the fields north of Kirkcaldy, far north of Edinburgh, a machine-gun post stands ready to repel Germans that never came. Built by our grandfathers, strong men who knew what they did was right, to me it shows an iron will, a determination to fight rather than give in — even when the enemy would have come so far and so much would had been lost before it ever saw them. It was built to enable men to fight and die in a war that would already have been lost by the time it reached them. I do not know if we could show such spirit now. Even if some of us could, surely we would ask ourselves: what exactly are we fighting *for*: what is there in Britain that needs to be preserved?

It is not a comfortable question.

I haven't given up on my country, though the temptation to do so is felt strongly by my fellow young Britons who are emigrating at an alarming rate.[1] I believe that change for the better is still possible. We must be clear in saying who must take responsibility.

Who Should Act?

There is a preconception in modern Britain that change must be led by government. As I outlined in a previous chapter, I believe in a small government, active and powerful within its strictly defined and limited sphere. Generally speaking, societal moral judgments do not fall within that area. For government should steer the country's life — it should not row. Only citizens do that. Rather, I look to individuals in society to form a shared attitude to fault and exert

---

[1]   The 'big five' destination countries — Australia, Canada, New Zealand, South Africa and the United States — are *all* recording a record number of young immigrants from the UK.

moral pressure upon it. The fact that something is wrong with Britain does not mean that it is government's job to fix it. Indeed, it is this over-reliance on government that has led to some of this trouble in the first place, as government itself is often at fault, and as individuals have abdicated responsibility: they have asked not what they can do for society, but when is government going to get round to doing it for them.

Evidence for the undesirability of governmental over-activity is found even when new laws are not — in and of themselves — bad, in the uncertainty such activity creates. A genuinely free society has at its heart the certainty of the rule of law. But when (as now) government ministers casually introduce new laws, that seek fundamentally to change the way that society is run, at a rate apparently restricted only by their typing speed, that certainty is undermined. To paraphrase Madison, what good is the rule of law, if no man knows what the law will be tomorrow?

Furthermore, whilst willingness on the part of the British government to support moral opprobrium is both desirable and long overdue, this is an arena in which governments are not the most effective operators. Supportive peer attitude is empowering to the individual and makes them more likely to stand their moral ground when challenged by situations in their lives. It is more likely to affect what the individual actually thinks than government diktat. The spiral into the failures I've outlined hasn't, for the most part, been led by government, but rather by peer solidarity being eroded from within: it is probable that government *can't* fix this situation, even if it tried. Leaders can cast a vision for a better society, and they should. But there is no government bill that can enact a policy of decent behaviour.

In any case, when governments take a paternalistic view it might be thought to absolve individuals of responsibility they'd otherwise take. If the government tells me that it will take care of the environment, I'm less likely to do my part in the process of recycling or caring for nature around me. Similarly, if the government tells me that it's responsible for morality, I am less likely to interact proscriptively with individuals breaching my moral code: I am more likely to hope for government intervention, and shrug my shoulders when it does not appear.

So: it is natural that government should want to address problems it knows concern the public — and the fall of public morals, especially amongst the young, generates a great deal of concern in what is left of civil society. But sometimes, it would be more effective if government simply declared openly that these are problems that it cannot actually fix — that it is for the citizenry to heal itself. This is such a case.

Also, the breaching of government-imposed rules — of laws — always has an element of excitement, an innate appeal to the adventurous individual. Whilst this can also be true of breaches of a common moral code, I believe the latter to be less likely: respect for a moral stricture held by family or tribal members is more likely to be held by individuals than an innate respect for written law, given its immediacy and its status as promulgated by loved ones rather than the state. Some will always want to break social norms: the issue at hand is how to minimise that lobby, how to minimise its willingness to act on the compulsion, and how to minimise the effects when it does so act.

For all these reasons, this is an arena that depends on individuals for improvement: for change from the bottom up, rather than from the top-down.

We should also ask ourselves if we would want government to exercise control in this arena even if it could. The problems identified in this book are, by and large, things that are not illegal, but are unpleasant: graffiti, offensive manners, yobbery, teen disrespect for society. Where these things *are* illegal, for example the mass practices of underage drinking and smoking, it would involve a huge extension of the state's powers to tackle them given their current widespread nature. If we did ask the state to deal with these issues, the state would of necessity be overwhelmingly powerful.

The Role of Law

Increasingly, ours is a society governed by the letter of the law, rather than by a sense of what is right. But laws, and the 'rights' they give us, can't be the basis of morality, as they rest on the concepts of justice and injustice, rather than moral good. When in play, they *make* a misbehaving person change his behaviour, and his action is only what he must do, nothing more: the person claiming his right gets what he is entitled to according to the law, nothing more. There is no room in such analysis for moral good, and no credit for an individual for doing the right thing.

Instead, in forming a moral system, we should rely on the fact that people know, or should know, right from wrong, and understand basic human virtues.

Unfortunately, the legal framework seems increasingly to be the method by which society forms moral judgments. Morality in modern Britain is yielded by individuals to the state; increasingly, the state acts as moral arbiter and individuals are viewed (and view themselves) as amoral actors, shuttling between boundaries that are set by the state in the form of laws. Individuals ask, 'how far can I go before the state stops me? That determines what is right.' But the law should determine *outer* boundaries of behaviour, showing what behaviour is *so* bad that the state will intervene, rather than mark the line before which everything else is equally without fault.

This faith in the power of government is shared, at least in part, even by those that spearhead attempts to achieve recognition for quite how wrong our society has become. One whose diagnosis of British society is all but identical to mine writes,

> an enlightened government could help to revive ideas of responsibility, good and bad, guilt and innocence. This would greatly strengthen the position of the large number of citizens who still believe in self-discipline based on a common morality. It would help in the remoralization of our country.[2]

I agree that responsibility should be revived. I believe that those citizens that still believe in the great forgotten virtue of self-discipline, especially one based on a common morality, deserve support — indeed, such an attitude, supported by government, would yield huge societal benefits. I believe that the 'remoralization' of our country is a vital aim. But I do not believe that it is government's role to *initiate* it. Hitchens goes on to write,

> It would be pointless to try to deal with the rise in disorder solely through changes in the law and in police methods. A moral counter-revolution is needed. Practical reforms, however, would help such a counter-revolution to begin and hasten it once it had started, provided they were not attempted in isolation.[3]

We share the same aims, believe in the same fundamental goals for British society; nothing less than a revolution has occurred in the way we behave, in the way we *are*, and nothing less dramatic than a 'counter-revolution' can bring society back to the position we both fervently *hope* it can attain. But the ordering of events is reversed: rather than an enlightened government leading the counter-revolution, I believe that such a government will have to be *led*. Hitchens is a Straussian, wanting to use the government to promote virtue. Given all the problems with government involvement stated above, I am uncertain that this is possible. Since it may do damage rather than good, I want government to leave well alone. I believe that

---

[2] Peter Hitchens *The Abolition of Liberty* London 2003 pp. 15–16.
[3] Peter Hitchens op cit.

government can only *follow* such a moral agenda once it is given both the spur and the legitimacy to do so by popular opinion.

We must generate that opinion. Ourselves. No-one else will do it for us. It's up to you. Step up.

*   *   *

I have put my case without the irony and sardonic smile that characterise many that think like me who have already given up. I do not shrug or seek to hide my sadness: I lament what is happening to my country.

We can yet bring a halt to the miasma of decline in Britain, if only the great middle of our society is willing to take up its burden once again. When the central pillar collapses, the house falls down. But when it merely crumbles, it can — for a time — be repaired.

There may be readers of this work who see their society accurately described herein. To them, fellow unwilling witnesses to Britannia's withering, I ask: what are you doing about it?

The flaw in Hutber's premise when he wrote *The Decline and Fall of the Middle Class and How it Can Fight Back* was one unknowable in his time. He assumed that the middle class would *want* to fight back.

Don't you?

I am an exile in my own country, whose centuries-old traditions have been dismantled in moments. I am an exile in my own class, which should speak but remains silent, should act but only stands still. Perhaps you feel this way too.

I hope so.

Select Bibliography

An Anthology of Pieces from Early Editions of Encyclopaedia Britannica (London, 1963)

Anderson, Digby and Peter Mullen (eds.) *Faking It: The Sentimentalisation of Modern Society* (London, 1998)

Auden, W.H. *The Dyer's Hand & Other Essays* (London, 1963)

Brett, Judith *Australian Liberals and the Moral Middle Class: from Alfred Deakin to John Howard* (Cambridge, 2003)

Care, Jeffrey *The Observer: Sayings of the Eighties* (London, 1989)

de Botton, Alain *Status Anxiety* (London, 2004)

Field, Frank *Neighbours from Hell: the Politics of Behaviour* (London, 2003)

Gabb, Sean *Cultural Revolution, Culture War: The True Battle for Britain* London, 2003

Grierson, Edward *The Imperial Dream: British Commonwealth and Empire 1775-1969* (London, 1972)

Hitchens, Peter *The Abolition of Britain* (London, 1999)

Hitchens, Peter *The Abolition of Liberty: the Decline of Order and Justice in England* (London, 2004: revised edition)

Hutber, Patrick *The Decline and Fall of the Middle Class and How it Can Fight Back* (London, 1976)

Kelling, George L. and Ronald Corbett 'This Works: Preventing and Reducing Crime' *Civic Bulletin*, No 32 March 2003: Center for Civic Innovation at the Manhattan Institute

Kirkegaard, Søren *Fear and Trembling* Trans. Alastair Hannay (London, 1985)

Morton Blum, John *The Republican Roosevelt* (Cambridge, MA 1977)

Patten, John *Things to Come: The Tories in the 21st Century* (London, 1995)

Peck, M. Scott *The Road Less Travelled* (New York, 1978)

Phillips, Melanie *All Must Have Prizes* (London 1997, revised ed)

Scruton, Roger *England: An Elegy* (London, 2001)

Tawney, R.H. *Equality* (London, 1931)

SOCIETAS: essays in political and cultural criticism

Contemporary public debate has been impoverished by two competing trends. On the one hand the increasing commercialization of the media has meant that in-depth commentary has given way to the ten-second soundbite. On the other hand the explosion of scholarly knowledge has led to intense specialization, so that academic discourse has ceased to be comprehensible. As a result writing on politics and culture is either superficial or baffling.

This was not always so — especially for politics. The high point of the English political pamphlet was the seventeenth century, when a number of small printer-publishers responded to the political ferment of the age with an outpouring of widely-accessible pamphlets and tracts. Indeed Imprint Academic publishes facsimile C17th. reprints under the banner 'The Rota'.

In recent years the tradition of the political pamphlet has declined—with most publishers rejecting anything under 100,000 words. The result is that many a good idea ends up drowning in a sea of verbosity. However the digital press makes it possible to re-create a more exciting age of publishing. *Societas* authors are all experts in their own field, but the essays are for a general audience. Each book can be read in an evening. The books are available retail at the price of £8.95/$17.90 each, or on bi-monthly subscription for only £5/$10. Details: **imprint-academic.com/societas**

IMPRINT ACADEMIC, PO Box 200, Exeter, EX5 5YX, UK
Tel: (0)1392 841600   Fax: (0)1392 841478   sandra@imprint.co.uk
imprint-academic.com/societas

SOCIETAS

essays in political and cultural criticism

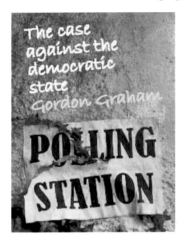

The Case Against the Democratic State

Gordon Graham

We are now so used to the state's pre-eminence in all things that few think to question it. This essay contends that the gross imbalance of power in the modern state is in need of justification, and that democracy simply masks this need with an illusion of popular sovereignty. Although the arguments are accessible to all, it is written within the European philosophical tradition. The author is Professor of Moral Philosophy at the Uniiversity of Aberdeen. 96 p., £8.95/$17.90

The Snake that Swallowed its Tail

Mark Garnett

Liberal values are the hallmark of a civilised society. Yet they depend on an optimistic view of the human condition, Stripped of this essential ingredient, liberalism has become a hollowed-out abstraction. Tracing its effects through the media, politics and the public services, the author argues that hollowed-out liberalism has helped to produce our present discontent. Unless we stop boasting about our values and try to recover their essence, liberal society will be crushed in the coils of its own contradictions. 96 pp., £8.95/$17.90

The Party's Over

Keith Sutherland

The book argues that the tyranny of the modern political party should be replaced by a mixed constitution in which advocacy is entrusted to an aristocracy of merit, and democratic representation is achieved via a jury-style lottery. 200 pp., £8.95/$17.90

●*'An extremely valuable contribution–a subversive and necessary read.'* **Graham Allen MP**, *Tribune*

● *'His analysis of what is wrong is superb . . . No one can read this book without realising that something radical, even revolutionary must be done.'* **Sir Richard Body**, *Salisbury Review*

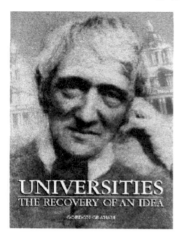

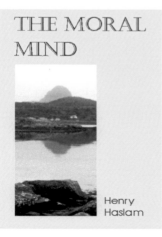

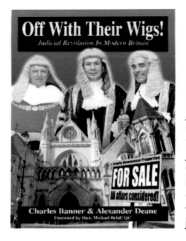

Off With Their Wigs!
Judicial revolution in modern Britain
Charles Banner & Alex Deane

In response to intense criticism of the Government for announcing their 2003 judicial reforms without holding any prior debate or consultation, the authors sought the views of constitutional experts – including judges, QCs, legal and political academics, commentators and MPs. Citing the interviewees at length, the book analyses the Government's proposals and looks at the various alternative models for appointing judges and for a new court of final appeal

160 pp., £8.95/$17.90 0907845843

Our Last Great Illusion
Rob Weatherill

This book aims to refute, primarily through the prism of modern psychoanalysis and postmodern theory, the notion of a return to nature, to holism, or to a pre-Cartesian ideal of harmony and integration. Far from helping people, therapy culture's utopian solutions may be a cynical distraction, creating delusions of hope. Yet solutions proliferate in the free market, to the precise degree that there are *no* solutions. This is why therapy is our last great illusion. Rob Weatherill lectures in psychoanalysis at Trinity College, Dublin and is a practitioner of 2years standing..

96 pp., £8.95/$17.90 0907845959

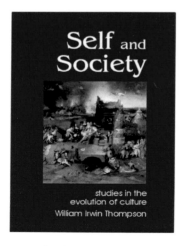

Self and Society
William Irwin Thompson

The book is comprised of a series of essays on the evolution of culture, dealing with topics including the city and consciousness, evolution of the afterlife, literary and mathematical archetypes, machine consciousness and the implications of 9/11 and the invasion of Iraq for the development of planetary culture.The author is a poet and cultural historian and the author of 16 books.

96 pp., £8.95/$17.90

sample chapters, reviews and TOCs: www.imprint-academic.com/societas